GIRL IN THE GOLD CAMP
A TRUE ACCOUNT OF AN ALASKA ADVENTURE, 1909–1910

Peggy Rouch Dodson at Eagle Creek in 1910 in her favorite hunting attire.

Girl in the Gold Camp
A True Account of an Alaska Adventure, 1909–1910

Peggy Rouch Dodson

Co-published by:

Beistline Enterprises

Epicenter Press
Fairbanks / Seattle

Epicenter Press
Fairbanks / Seattle

Epicenter Press Inc. is a regional press founded in Alaska whose interests include but are not limited to the arts, history, environment, and diverse cultures and lifestyles of the North Pacific and high latitudes. We seek both the traditional and innovative in publishing quality nonfiction tradebooks, contemporary art and photography giftbooks, and destination travel guides emphasizing Alaska, Washington, Oregon, and California.

Senior Editor: Lael Morgan
Researcher & Editorial Assistant: Rosalie L'Ecuyer
Book Design & Copy Editing: Sue Mitchell, Inkworks
Cover Design: Elizabeth Watson
Proofreaders: Lois Kelly, Christine Ummel
Maps: Scott Penwell
Printer: Best Books Manufacturing
Text © 1996 Peggy Rouch Dodson

ISBN 0-945397-53-4
Library of Congress Catalog Card Number: 94-084283

To order single copies of GIRL IN THE GOLD CAMP, mail $14.95 (Washington residents add $1.23 sales tax) plus $4 for priority mail shipping to: Epicenter Press, Box 82368, Kenmore, WA 98028.

Booksellers: Retail discounts are available from our distributor, Graphic Arts Center Publishing™, Box 10306, Portland, OR 97210. Phone 800-452-3032.

PRINTED IN CANADA
First Printing May 1996

10 9 8 7 6 5 4 3 2

TABLE OF CONTENTS

FOREWORD

As a vivacious girl of about sixteen, Peggy Rouch traveled to Alaska from California and lived for a year and a half with her aunt and uncles, Nellie and Ed and Alf Garner, at a frontier mining operation on Eagle Creek in Interior Alaska, which gave her first-hand information and knowledge to write her fascinating, down-to-earth story, *Girl in the Gold Camp: A True Account of an Alaska Adventure, 1909–1910.* At the time, the Garners were helping to set up the mining operation for Clarence Berry, a successful Klondike stampeder who later did well in oil exploration and development, resulting in the formation of the Berry Petroleum Company that continues to operate to the present day in California and in Alaska as the Eagle Creek Mining and Drilling Company.

Ed and Nellie Garner were associated with mining in the Eagle Creek area with Ed's brother, Alf Garner, until their deaths during the sinking of the *Princess Sophia* between Skagway and Juneau, Alaska, in 1918.

In the summer of 1987, Joyce and Bill Reece, daughter and son-in-law of Peggy Rouch Dodson, visited Central, Alaska, with this manuscript in hand. There, Patricia (Pat) Oakes read it and was very much impressed by the historical importance of the factual story.

Accordingly, Pat Oakes purchased all publishing rights to the manuscript and selected photos, with the copyright remaining with the author and family. The Circle District Museum was given the rights to use the manuscript for research only.

Unforeseen was the unexpected and sad passing of Patricia Oakes on November 22, 1993. She had begun editing the manuscript for publication and selecting photos to accompany the text.

Pat is to be highly commended for the editing work she began and for her foresight in recognizing the significance of Peggy's Alaska experience.

A miner and long-time resident of Circle, I became interested in the manuscript after I leased Garner mining sites on Eagle Creek from Eagle Creek Mining & Drilling Company, which continues to be involved in mining on the original Berry claims. The house lived in by Peggy and the Garners was on this property, and because of this I became well acquainted with Peggy and her family. Comparing Peggy's first-hand accounts of the experiences of Alaska pioneer miners with what I know about present-day mining methods and conditions has been a wonderful experience, and I've really enjoyed knowing Peggy.

On Pat Oakes's death I purchased the publishing rights to *Girl in the Gold Camp* with full concurrence of the author, Peggy Rouch Dodson, and Joyce and Bill Reece.

Also of interest in the appendix is material from writer James A. Michener about his honored frontispiece photograph of Peggy Rouch's aunt Nellie Garner in his novel *Journey*, copyrighted in 1988. Michener discussed the importance of Nellie Garner to the writing of his book *Journey,* about the adventures of people headed for the riches of the Klondike gold fields. Also included in the appendix is an excerpt from Melanie J. Mayer's *Klondike Women: True Tales of the 1897–1898 Gold Rush,* which details Ed and Nell's trip on the Edmonton Trail.

Here, now, is the story of her Alaskan interlude by Peggy Rouch Dodson. Best wishes for good reading.

—Earl H. Beistline
Fairbanks, Alaska

PREFACE
WHO IS PEGGY ROUCH DODSON?

PEGGY was born Bertha Pearl Rouch on April 9, 1893, the youngest of four children of Frank Rouch and Julia Garner Rouch.Bertha was the only girl; her brothers were Claude, Alva, and Ruby. She preferred her nickname, Peggy, and ever since has been recognized as Peggy. Her parents owned a 160-acre ranch near Kingsburg, California. She enjoyed the ranch life, exploring the land, riding her pony, learning to shoot, and having numerous friends. Her mother died when Bertha was three years old. At first placed in the care of an aunt who died shortly thereafter, she was later brought up by her father with the help of housekeepers. The girl attended the Clay School with her brothers and completed two years at Kingsburg Joint Union High School. In the meantime, her father had remarried, and her stepmother was most inconsiderate to Peggy.

In the early spring of 1909, Peggy's two uncles, Ned (sometimes called Ed) and Alf Garner, and Ned's wife, Nell, were in Kingsburg preparing to return to Alaska with supplies for their mining operations on Eagle Creek in the Circle Mining District. Nell was like a mother to Peggy, and accordingly, she asked Peggy's father if her family could take the girl to Alaska with them. Peggy wished to get away from the frustration caused by her stepmother and was thrilled to go to a frontier land with people who loved her.

Nell had been born Nellie Paddock in Wisconsin, but she was raised in Hanford, California, near where Peggy grew up.

Like Peggy, she had come from a close farming family—one brother and five sisters—and because she missed them and had no children of her own, there could have been no doubt in Peggy's mind that she was wanted by her handsome young aunt.

So began Peggy's life and activities in a frontier mining camp, living under pioneering conditions in Interior Alaska and enjoying the four Alaska seasons with their extremes of winter weather, northern lights, and long, warm, sunny summers.

While at the Eagle Creek Mine, she agreed to work with Nell every morning doing whatever needed to be done—washing, cooking, cleaning, gardening, etc. In the afternoons she was free to hunt, hike, wade, write, and visit her friend Helen Callahan. Happy in the out-of-doors, Peggy became an excellent shot and brought many ptarmigan back for dinner. She became highly respected by the miners and all who knew her, but in 1910 one of her friends influenced her to go back to California and continue her education. During her Alaska residence, she had three proposals of marriage but did not accept any of them; there continued to be the boy back home.

Her experiences in Alaska resulted in her writing *Girl in the Gold Camp* many years later from memory and her diary.

The story, which covers a time and place about which virtually nothing else has been written, is an excellent contribution to the history of a phase of early day Alaska pioneering, experienced by a young lady who knew and remembered it well.

—Patricia Oakes

INTRODUCTION
THE GARNERS AND THE BERRYS
COME TO ALASKA

THE discovery of rich placer gold in the Yukon Territory, Canada, in 1896 by George Carmack stimulated the Klondike Gold Rush of 1898, an event that inspired thousands of people to set out for the Northland.

Alf Garner (Alfred Renfro Garner, born May 21, 1871, in California) was one of the hundreds of stampeders who hiked over Chilkoot Pass from Skagway, bound for the gold fields near Dawson. He made the grueling trip on foot, carrying a heavy pack and enduring many hardships. Unsuccessful in locating a paying claim there, he put his good marksmanship to practical use and hunted game, which meant fresh meat to sell to miners. Later he went to Nome on Alaska's northwest coast and from there to Eagle Creek near Circle City, where at last he found the foot of his rainbow. He wrote immediately to his brother Ned (Jefferson Edward Garner, born January 8, 1869) and Ned's wife, Nellie, begging them to join him.

Without hesitation they sold their farm, tools, animals, and household goods and set out on the long trip in 1897. Advised that the old White Pass Trail from Skagway would be hard for Aunt Nellie, they went up through Canada to Edmonton and Calgary, both only struggling outposts. Here transportation ended.

Aunt Nellie was one of the first white women to pass through these small settlements, one of about twenty-one women among 1,500 stampeders on various branches of the Edmonton Trail.

There was a party of men planning to walk across the mountains to the Yukon, and the Garners expected to join them. Some of the men objected to allowing a frail-looking woman to join them. A meeting was held where arguments got so hot that the party split, with the "pro" group inviting the young couple to join them. This group decided to pool their provisions and to cook and eat together.

Auntie Nell was a durable and uncomplaining traveler. She also loved to cook, and the men in her group were more than anxious to do all the heavy camp chores so that she and Uncle Ned could prepare the meals.

Traveling about the same distance each day, the two groups often made camp near each other. After several days of seeing how well Auntie got along and of smelling her cooking, two of the men from the "anti" camp approached the Garner camp. Auntie was embarrassed but Uncle Ned was adamant that they get down on their knees before her and beg to be allowed to join the "pro" group.

However, prolonged spells of bad weather dogged them all—provisions grew shorter, and finally to save their lives, all were forced to turn back. The trail they had chosen, known as the "Poor Folks Way," turned out to be one of the most difficult routes to the gold fields. The Garners went back to California.

In 1900, the railroad from Skagway to Whitehorse was complete. By that time Alf Garner had done very well (mining, hunting, and perhaps gambling) and was able to send funds so Ned and Nellie could ride comfortably to Whitehorse, Yukon Territory, Canada. From there they traveled by river steamer to Circle City, Alaska, where the three of them had a grand reunion.

In the years that followed, the Garners were a devoted trio, living, working, or traveling happily together. The claims they staked provided well for them, but because they lacked the capital to fully develop them, they sold out to Clarence Berry in 1906, then stayed on to manage the venture.

Alf Garner had undoubtedly met Clarence Berry and his wife, Ethel, in Dawson, when they were struggling to make their fortunes. Alf's favorite story was of Berry, who had prospected Fortymile country for years without success, learning of the new strike at Bonanza while tending bar for Bill McPhee and immediately running as fast as he could to stake his claim, which would prove the richest in the fields.

Berry invested his gold earnings in a successful California oil venture, then returned to the Far North to buy up some of the richest claims in the Circle Mining District, where he would succeed again, and his friends, the Garners, with him.

—Earl H. Beistline

EDITOR'S ACKNOWLEDGEMENTS

I would like to thank George O'Leary and Fred Wilkinson of Central, Ed and Clayton Lapp of Eagle Creek, and Madoline Wilkinson of Seattle, Washington, for providing background for this book. I am also grateful for the help of Lee Alder, Mary Nordale, Judy Lampi, and Melanie McCann of Fairbanks; Frank and Mary Warren of Central and Fairbanks; Bob Casey of Hogg 'Em Gulch; Dr. William Wood, president emeritus, University of Alaska Fairbanks; and Audrey Oaks of Avoca, Arkansas, for working with us. Melanie Mayer's gracious permission for use of her material from *Klondike Women: True Tales of the 1897–98 Gold Rush* is greatly appreciated. The Circle District Historical Society was generous in allowing us to use its research collection. And our special thanks to Bill and Joyce Reece, without whom this project would never have gotten off the ground.

—Earl H. Beistline

Author's Appreciation

I express my thanks and appreciation to the following people for their confidence and assistance in following through and publishing my manuscript, *Girl in the Gold Camp*. My Alaska experience with relatives who gave me love, participating in pioneer life in a mining camp, becoming acquainted with new friends, learning about Alaska geography, living in extremes of Alaska's winter and summer weather, and taking time to consider my own life and objectives, continue to be precious memories that give me happiness.

Joyce & Bill Reece (daughter and son-in-law)
Patricia Ann Oakes
Earl H. Beistline

—Peggy Rouch Dodson
November 1994

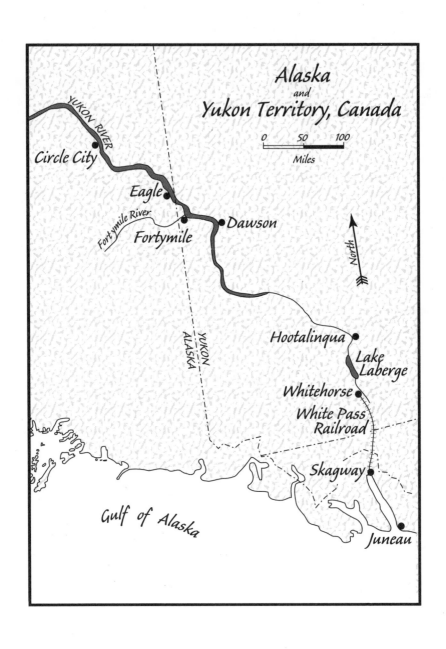

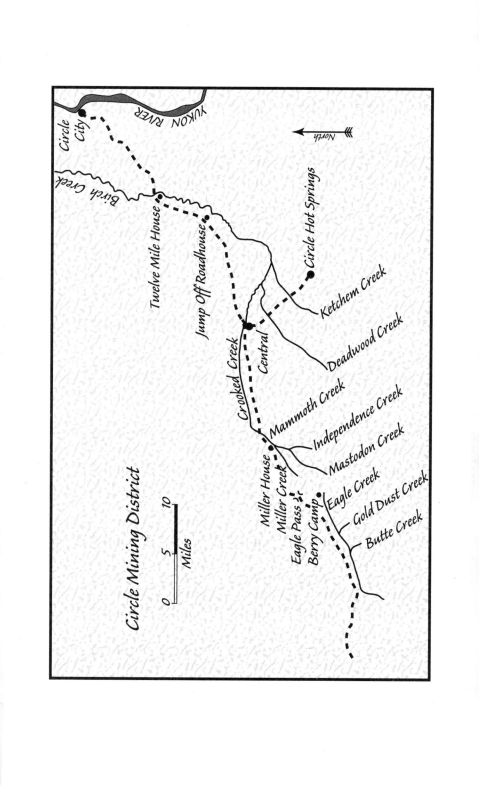

Circle Mining District

Chapter 1

MY DECISION TO GO TO ALASKA

AFTER my mother died, my father remarried, and my relationship with my stepmother, Lily, was not good from a mother/daughter standpoint. This was especially so when I felt that my mother's memory, revered by all who had known her for many years, was being criticized.

My deceased mother's brothers, Alfred and Edward Garner, and the latter's wife, Nellie, spent the winter of 1908 and 1909 in Fresno, California, near my home. When spring came and they were about to return to their mining operation on Eagle Creek, Alaska, they begged my father to allow me to go with them.

It was a few weeks before my sixteenth birthday. My father gave his consent but wisely left the decision of whether or not to accept the invitation to me. On one side of my quandary was leaving my beloved father and brothers, two at home, constant companions, and another in San Francisco. There was a high school sweetheart, my girl chum, a pony to ride, and the dear old ranch on which to roam.

On the other side of the question was the prospect of travel and an exciting new life with these well-loved relatives who were glamour personified to all of the family. Successful in their search for gold, they were able to enjoy many comforts and some small luxuries and were most generous with thoughtful gifts for all of their two families. They were offering me almost a new world, but even more importantly, loving care and a peaceful home.

Alaska! An opportunity for a refreshing, closer association with my uncles and aunt. I would go to Alaska!

Chapter 2

CALIFORNIA TO WHITEHORSE, YUKON TERRITORY, CANADA

O N April 9, 1909, my birthday, I departed from home by horse and buggy for Fresno, where I joined Alf, Ed, and Nell for our trip to San Francisco by train.

Uncle Alf was lean and long-legged and above medium height. The tall black hats he wore seemingly added inches. His hair was dark, as was his thin mustache, trimmed to a fine point. The unusual vision of his deep gray-blue eyes allowed him to discover game animals at a great distance. His nose was large, a family trait, and although he was quiet and reserved, he enjoyed being with people. He wore a gold nugget chain across his vest, and a slow smile revealed gold fillings in his teeth. He was adept at rolling his own Bull Durham cigarettes with one hand and smoked them continually. He was generous to a fault with those he loved, but slow to forgive an injustice.

Uncle Ed was two years older than his brother, shorter in stature and unlike him in almost every way. His wavy light brown hair, merry blue eyes, and constant smile gave him a boyish, mischievous look. He wore and joked about his wide suspenders and plug hat—the style at that time, but clothes in general were not of too much importance to him. He was kind and thoughtful and had the rare faculty of finding a comical side to almost every situation. He adored his little wife and cared not a whit if the whole world knew it. Although he was rather short in stature, she had to look up to him—as indeed she did anyway.

Aunt Nellie was not a great beauty, but she was very pretty. She had regular features, a tiny mouth, and two deep dimples. Her hair, which was always beautifully combed, was dark brown, as were her large eyes. She was slender and, in dress and manner, utterly feminine. She never went to bed without a thorough face creaming and kid curler hair treatment.

I learned too soon that fatigue, lateness of the hour, nothing excused me from a similar routine. Auntie never scolded—just took it for granted that I would fit the mold and saw to it that I had all of the necessary tools and cosmetics for the chore. For a country girl who had grown up motherless since the toddler age with three older brothers under the casual care of housekeepers, following this rigid routine regularly was sometimes rough. However, I adored Auntie, and it warmed my mother-hungry heart to be treated like a much-loved daughter.

We stayed in San Francisco about one week, during which time my aunt and uncles really showed me the town. It was there that I saw for the first time a woman smoking—shocking to me!

From San Francisco we went by ship to Seattle. En route I encountered seasickness and when Uncle Ned asked me if I wanted to die, I said, "Yes." We stayed in Seattle one week, during which time we obtained all the supplies we needed for our Alaska home, including a fur coat and parka for me. Before we left Seattle, my new family met (by appointment) several Alaska friends who planned to make the trip "inside" with us.

Their dear friend Rass, who had been spending the winter with his mother in the East, was the first to greet us. R. Rassmussen, who was affectionately called "Rass" by all who knew him, had lived and worked with the Garners for several years.[1] He was Danish, and was short and square with broad shoulders and a shock of black hair like that of his heavy mustache. He was good-natured and smiling. I grew to have great respect and admiration for Rass through the many months that followed. M. Clark, the eldest of the friends, was known only as "Clark." He was a Greek—about sixty years old but very agile and strong in spite of his years. He had short, curly black hair, peppered with gray, that stuck out in all directions. He seldom wore a hat except in the coldest weather. His large Roman nose lost its dimensions when a wide smile revealed several gold teeth. Like Rass, Clark was loved by all, and every one of us received many large and small courtesies from him during our association.

Jim Woods was a rotund, middle-aged man with a jolly disposition, reddish complexion, and hair of the same tone. He was a bit above medium height, deliberate and slow in his movements. He looked after his nephew Andy with fatherly devotion. Jim hoped that by taking Andy on this trip, he might change his nephew's objective of becoming an undertaker.

Andy looked a bit like Jim but only in his coloring and red hair. He was light in weight, shorter than his uncle, and his pale complexion emphasized his many freckles. He looked older than his twenty years, perhaps because of the plug hat he wore. Andy was reserved and shy, willing to let others make decisions—but an obliging aider or abettor.

Bill Cressman, who was a little older than Andy Woods, was an athletic-looking chap who had been saving since his early teens to make it to Alaska. He had found our group by making his way to Seattle, asking questions at the hotels and steamship offices. Bill was strong and not un-handsome. He had unruly brown hair, and his clothes often looked their seeming unimportance to him. He loved to play harmless pranks but proved to be a responsible and good-natured companion to us all.[2]

Sam Warren, our man of many talents, was medium height with dark hair and complexion. Although he weighed only one hundred and fifty pounds, he was muscular and strong. Sam was the quiet type but always seemed to have some solution for any emergency, as did my uncles Alf and Ned.[3]

Our group departed Seattle on the steamer *Cottage City*.[4] The boat trip through Alaska's Inside Passage was great. I played the piano a little bit. An elderly man had a violin, and he said, "Young lady, you get up here and help me." We played for dancing. I remember that the *Cottage City* stopped at several communities to unload freight and/or passengers en route to Skagway, including Wrangell and Treadwell, where there was a world-class hard rock gold mine and a fish cannery.

On the steamer between Seattle and Skagway, we became acquainted with an old seaman, Captain Geer. The captain introduced us to his daughter, a young woman of about thirty. When he learned of our destination, he privately asked my uncles if she might join us and go as far as a certain camp on the Yukon, promising to pay well for her passage.[5]

Miss Geer was not unattractive, but no beauty by any standards. She had dark hair, fair skin, and hazel eyes, and was rather slender in build. She was reserved but affable, and after a family conference of the four of us, we decided to take her along. The addition of Miss Geer swelled our numbers to eleven.

When we arrived at Skagway, we learned that there would be a three-day wait for the train to Whitehorse. We were happy to stretch our legs. On the day following our arrival, Bill, Andy, Miss Geer, and I set out to hike up on the mountain behind the town to the source of its water supply. A well-used trail made the two miles seem shorter because of the ever-changing views of the snowy mountains and the blue-green Pacific. The water supply proved to be only a very small lake fed by springs. But the rock formations and interesting plant life, plus the good exercise, made the climb worthwhile.

The outing had a pleasant interruption when on the way down the mountainside we met a garrulous old man near the foot of the trail. Crippled with age and rheumatism, he was limping along, carefully turning many of the smaller stones in the path with his knobby cane. When he "howdy"-ed us in a friendly way, we stopped and started asking him questions about Alaska. The old man was happy to talk, and since he was among the earlier gold prospectors, had many tales to tell. He had questions of his own about the States. When Andy said he was from Iowa, the old man stroked his straggly beard and said reverently, "Ioway. Ioway, that's right where I was born. I'm a-goin' back there some day." He added brightly, "When I get me a mite more pay dirt. Got me a little mine over near Dawson—come here every winter—more folks around. Don't pay much, my diggins, but I make a good livin'. Ioway, Ioway," he repeated longingly. "Be good to see my folks again—ain't many left." Without saying goodbye, he got to his feet suddenly and started off, muttering, "Ioway, Ioway."

By evening before we left Skagway, all baggage had been carefully sorted, trunks packed, and only those necessities for the trip into the Interior left to be taken with us. The big trunks and large boxes were bonded through from this point in U.S. Alaska to Circle, so we would not pay duties going through Yukon Territory, Canada.

Auntie packed our gay spring hats away. We had bought and worn them in San Francisco during the week of shopping there. On the few rainless days in Seattle, we had worn them again and now (I thought) we had worn them for the last time.

The shrill whistle blew, the conductor yelled, "All aboard," and we were on our way to Whitehorse, 120 miles away. We climbed up and up—there were snow-covered or -capped mountains on both sides of the track. Masses of frothy clouds softened their craggy outlines against an azure sky. The little train[6] puffed around hairpin turns, through green forests, and along deep ravines. We passed a huge rock with a small cross near it, and the conductor told us that a workman had been crushed by its weight when the railroad was being built. Since the massive stone could not be moved, it became a monument to the worker's memory.

When we crossed a beautiful bridge 250 feet high at Dead Horse Gulch, our accommodating conductor explained that during the height (and worst) of the 1898 stampede, hundreds of overburdened horses and mules, exhausted and starved by heedless owners, died here.

At Summit, twenty miles from Skagway, we had climbed 2,900 feet. This was not only the crest of the pass, but the international boundary between Alaska and Canada.

A Canadian customs officer came aboard to inspect our luggage. I was a bit miffed, much to the amusement of my family, when he went through my suitcases, briefly disturbing all of my belongings—lingerie, toilet articles, cosmetics—precious trappings such as I had never owned before. There was some argument over my fur jacket. Finally, it was settled that it was not brand-new and we did not have to pay duty on it. After all, it had been worn—worn on every possible occasion from the day of its purchase in San Francisco!

After we left Summit, the scenery was even more beautiful. We could see countless mountain peaks, and it seemed like dozens of blue and green lakes were scattered in all directions.

At Whitehorse we got accommodations for us all at a two-story log hotel and settled ourselves comfortably in rooms around the balcony upstairs. We lost no time in getting a good look at the famous Yukon River. It was frozen solid, and it seemed that everyone was betting on the day, hour, and minute that the "breakup" would come. The men in our group had been idle during the winter and were anxious to get back to work. The river steamers would not start their seasonal runs until the entire channel was open. Lake Laberge, through which a tributary of the Yukon passed, never thawed until sometime after the river ice went out, so that the only way to reach the Interior at this season was to go by small boat down the river, portaging across the frozen lake.

Traveling thus far so compatibly and enjoying the good fellowship among us all, our group decided to have a common "kitty" (food fund) and to travel and camp together.

Our first evening in Whitehorse was spent in serious planning for the eventualities ahead. Although hundreds of other people had made it safely down the river, only Uncle Alf, Rass, and Clark in our party had gone by this way. They realized that a more comfortable and safer journey would result from thorough preparedness. There were risks and hazards, they said, but to those greenhorns among us it was an exciting prospect.[7]

It was decided that three boats would be necessary to carry us all, along with our light luggage, bed rolls, camping equipment, guns, and food. Besides these things, they planned to buy three sleds with steel runners and canvas for three sails. When I asked innocently what in the world for, they answered seriously that when we came to Lake Laberge, the boats would be lifted each on a sled, a sail hoisted, and we would sail over the frozen lake. How I laughed! This was almost as bad as the tall tale about Alaska mosquitoes being one inch long—I surely didn't believe this one!

Boards for boat building were available at a sawmill nearby, and tar, nails, and other supplies were to be had at a general store. Several of the men set to work immediately. Others brought two small tents and two tarpaulins for rainy weather—and three sleds and canvas for three sails!

Aunt Nellie and Clark made food lists and ordered all provisions for cooking and eating.

It was May now, and as we were getting farther north and it was nearer midsummer and the midnight sun, there was plenty of time each day for work and for play at the hotel in the evening. Pushing the dining tables and chairs back to the walls gave us ample room to dance. Our genial hosts, a jolly couple, kept the phonograph going and joined in our fun. They even came to my rescue in a pillow fight when Uncle Ned and Rass were trying to force me to say "Uncle."

While the men worked daytimes, they whistled or sang, for were they not on their way home or to meet adventure?

Auntie and I wrote endless "wish you were heres," watched the men at work, or walked around the small town. We looked forward to our camp outing, and I made countless trips along the riverbank to see if there were cracks in the ice.

Miss Geer, our mysterious traveling companion, had very little luggage (much to Auntie's concern—not even a hat and gloves!) so that her personal preparations for the last lap of her journey were brief. We had asked no personal questions about her past, present, or future, and she had offered no information. Clark, being the oldest man in our group, had joked that if she was looking for a husband, surely this good-looking lot of bachelors, seven in all, should be enough for her to choose from. She either accompanied Auntie and me on our small tours or read the novels and magazines at the hotel.

The boats were soon completed, all supplies collected or in order, and the river was still frozen. A group of us took a hike up to Miles Canyon and to Whitehorse Rapids. We thought the canyon with its rocky walls beautiful. The rapids looked dangerous, as no doubt they were, for many unlucky prospectors had drowned trying to pass through them. A fine bridge now spans Miles Canyon, bypassing the rapids. In an earlier day, Jack London had fearlessly brought many boats safely through these rapids, making a few dollars for himself and saving many lives from the treacherous water that foamed through the narrow pass in summer.

Alas, the long-expected breakup came and we did not get to see the very beginning. About two o'clock one morning, Uncle Ed pounded on the wall that separated our bedrooms. "The breakup, Peggy. The breakup!" he shouted. "Listen!"

Eerie sounds were coming from the river: great muffled explosions, harsh grinding noises high in tone, descending the scale into moaning undertones, and sharp shots as from a miniature cannon. The discordant symphony built up toward a mighty climax, a climax that never reached its apex, but dissolved into a tympanic arrangement of CRASH! CRACK! BOOM! It was as if the angry river, heaving mightily, had split the thick ice armor on its back and was shouting in exultation! There was little sleep the remainder of the night as I lay tense and listening to this fanfare of spring, opening night, as it were, of a play about beautiful, strange Alaska. And I was part of the audience!

As soon as it was light, those among us to whom this was a new experience dressed warmly and hurried to the river to see what was happening. We were all a bit disappointed not to have seen the first crack in the ice, but the spectacle had barely started.

Massive, irregular blocks of ice were loosed from grotesque piles that reared crazily in the river. These hurried down the muddy current only to be stopped by other huge chunks that blocked their way. More and larger pieces flung themselves into the mass, making a temporary jam. Then a lone block cleared a way for itself and nudged the side of a jam in passing. The jolt loosened its parts and away they all swirled to join the seemingly endless train of white shapes moving out of sight. Where the riverbanks were low, great long ledges of ice were piled along the edge where they had been pushed haphazardly.

We were all so fascinated watching the fantastic spectacle that we could scarcely believe it when Uncle Ed came from the hotel to say it was lunch time. We had missed breakfast entirely!

Chapter 3

WHITEHORSE TO DAWSON AND CIRCLE CITY, ALASKA

ONLY a few days after the main channel of the river was ice-free, we were ready and anxious to get on our way. We had explored nearly every nook and cranny of Whitehorse, the boats had been tested and declared seaworthy, all supplies were at hand, and we were ready to stow our gear and be off. Both weight and bulk of everything were considered in its division.

Clark and Rass were taking Miss Geer in their boat, and Sam and Jim were responsible for the tenderfeet—Andy and Bill. We all had a good laugh when Clark and Bill went back to the hotel for something they said they had forgotten. Bill came back carrying a gallon ice cream freezer, and Clark proudly carried a "start" of sourdough he had begged from the hotel cook!

Much to my disgust, Auntie brought along two sunbonnets. I could look back to the time when I was six, instead of sixteen, when my father sewed a sunbonnet on my head as a reminder that it must be worn to keep the hot valley sun from getting me all tanned! Shades of Palm Beach! However, the glare from the water, intensified by many snowbanks along the way, was so bad that a sunbonnet proved a welcome protection. In spite of this being a camp-out, our nightly beauty routine must never be neglected, and much of the daytime Auntie and I wore gloves. Her idea, not mine!

Miss Geer wore an old hat of Clark's and managed somehow to keep her few white blouses and long dark skirts clean without the long, enveloping aprons Auntie insisted I wear when in camp.

One early mid-May morning, with wishes of "Godspeed" from the friendly hotel people, we pushed and slid our boats into the Yukon. The current was strong and we floated off smartly. The men rowed only enough to keep the boats in midstream. It was my job to manipulate the "sweep"—a long, strong slat of wood, cut like an oar except that it had a long handle. It was handled from a notch cut into the back rest on the stern. Pulling on it helped steer the heavily laden boat in the direction we wanted to go.

For Auntie's safety, if need arose, a rope handhold on either end of the seat in the prow was a thoughtful addition by Sam. He had added one on Clark's boat for Miss Geer also.

We were all so keyed up with excitement and joyful anticipation of the ride before us that there was much banter and shouting as the three boats stayed as close together as safety would allow.

About ten o'clock the first morning, a fire was built in the camp stove and the pipe adjusted firmly. Soon smoke was spiraling gustily in a gray plume as we sped gaily along, while a kettle of coffee brewed. We found a good-sized cooking pot more dependable while we were moving along than a coffeepot. How good hot coffee tasted and what fun Auntie had passing it out as the rowers maneuvered to get near her outstretched hand.

At midday we found a likely spot to pull into shore to eat lunch and to stretch our legs. By hurrying my lunch, I had time to search for small, unusual rock specimens for a collection in the making. After our lunch period, each washed his own dishes in the river, and we pushed off again for another three or four hours. Our night camp was chosen in the vicinity of trees, as conifer boughs were used for our beds.

Before we left Whitehorse a schedule of camp duties had been worked out so that each one knew his part of the responsibilities. There were wood and boughs to be cut, water to carry, and food to be prepared for us all. Aunt Nellie, Clark, and Uncle Ed did the cooking, with others willing and anxious to do the necessary cleaning up. As far as possible, everyone finished working at the same time. Miss Geer and I soon found that our last chore before bedtime was to pull a chunk of wood, a rock, or a heavy boot out of the layer of boughs in our respective beds! We learned to get even by filching various items of the suspected pranksters' clothing and tying them in knots or sewing them in many fine seams.

Each morning we rose early, ate a hearty breakfast, and were out on the river so that we made very good time.

When we reached the first rough water of any consequence, I was very uneasy. So many tales had been told of boats that had been wrecked and occupants drowned that I wanted to scream. Both uncles and Auntie became very quiet, and I could sense a tenseness in us all.

As we plunged into the jumping, frothing cascade, I misunderstood a signal from Uncle Alf and turned the sweep in the wrong direction. For a sickening interval we half-changed our course, and the helpless craft very nearly capsized.

Uncle Alf yelled, "Turn it the other way!" With all of my strength I reversed the sweep. Both uncles pulled mightily on the oars, and after an eternity we came out of a horrible spin, straightened out, and plunged ahead into safe water. I was shaking, thoroughly frightened and near tears, but no one said a word as we looked back to see our companions come safely through the danger.

That night when we camped we celebrated our safe run of the rapids by making ice cream in our precious freezer. It was easy to find ice. We carried ice cream salt, and with canned milk, dried eggs, sugar, and flavoring—and so many willing hands to crank the freezer—it was no trick at all to make a gallon of ice cream. We licked the pot and looked forward to the next gallon.

Soon we came to frozen Lake Laberge. It was thirty miles long and five miles wide, a flat white expanse that looked limitless. There was not the slightest stir of a breeze! How I laughed—but not for long.

It was soon evident that a little thing like a windless day would not deter our progress. The boats were pulled up on the lake ice, and each one was loaded on the sled. Working on ours first because it carried the stove and most readily available food, the men fastened rope loops on each side, and all but Auntie bent to the task of pulling the boat-loaded sled toward the far end of the lake. About 300 yards had been covered when Uncle Alf called a halt. The men unfastened the pulling ropes from the sled, and leaving Auntie and Clark to cook lunch, we walked back to the other boats. These were brought up in the same way and by the time we had gotten the last one up to the others it was lunch time. We were a hungry crew. We always carried a small supply of wood in our boat with the stove, and we were thankful for the hot meal.

The distance to the end of the lake looked very discouraging, but we knew we must keep going, as a prospect of a night on the ice was not especially agreeable. Bill filched one of our dish towels and printed on it in big black letters, "DAWSON OR BUST." As soon as we had finished eating, we hurried to put our lunch gear away. We had just lifted the precious little stove back to its place when Uncle Alf spotted the dog teams of some Indian freighters crossing the lake some distance away. There was a great hullabaloo of shouting and arm-waving before the freighters discovered us and stopped. Almost at once they turned their teams and drove over to us. Luckily some of their wide flat sleds were empty; our boats and sleds were hoisted up on them. We all found our seats in our respective boats and away we went—sailing over Lake Laberge—but not with sails! Each day brought new sights, new experiences. One morning as we floated serenely along, Uncle Alf's telescopic eyes spotted a big brown bear high up on the hillside. Away we all paddled as quickly as possible to the shore. The men who thought the hillside climb not worth the effort stayed with us girls and the boats. The hunters fanned out across a sizeable area and were soon lost to sight among the trees.

We waited anxiously. Uncle had noted that the bear was a big one. Suppose something should go wrong. There was not a doctor in miles should we need one. At last we heard several rifle shots, and some time later the triumphant hunters returned with a large chunk of bear meat. We cooked and cooked that dark red meat, but it was strong, tough, and dry. The bear had not long been out of his winter hibernation and, having used all of his fat, his meat was in poor condition.

There had been many comments about Five Finger Rapids. As we approached them, I made sure that no part of passing them would be my responsibility. The sweep was too long and unwieldy, anyway, they said. There were three large groups of solid rock formations in the riverbed, dividing it into separate channels through which the river rushed madly. We took the right channel, and I was thoroughly frightened as we drove into the dark, swirling water. We went through so fast there was only a glimpse of the somber rocks that towered above our heads. Just after we got through, boat and all seemed to drop under us to a lower level and we shot out into smooth water again. "How did you like that, Peggy?" someone called. I could only swallow.

One day we saw smoke curling out of a substantial-looking log cabin near the riverbank. Jim Woods had been wishing for light bread and he begged us to stop and see if the cabin owner would sell us a loaf. He opined that Clark's sourdough biscuits and flapjacks had been good, but—anyway, he liked light bread. So we landed, and he trudged off to be greeted by an announcing pack of barking dogs. Ten minutes later he came back to the boats, triumphantly carrying a large brown loaf of fresh bread. After some coaxing, we finally learned that he had paid seventy-five cents for the treasure. Bread in Seattle was then five cents a loaf! Poor Woods—the bread was treated as community property, and he sighed ruefully as we ate the last crumb for supper.

When we reached Dawson, I was thrilled to learn that although we would not stay overnight there, there would be time enough to look around, as well as to buy fresh supplies. We saw only a few people in the town itself, and a storekeeper's face wore a look of disbelief when we answered his question, "How did you get here?" He was amazed and said that most women coming by the river had leatherlike complexions. "How come you are so white?" he asked, indicating Auntie and me. Uncle Ned chuckled, "They both wore sunbonnets and we held umbrellas over them."

Had he seen Miss Geer, who had not entered the store with us, he would not have been doubtful that she came by the river. She found a man's hat very hard to keep in place when the wind blew, and was indeed tanned.

As the loose boards on the wooden sidewalks creaked under our rambling footsteps, Uncle Alf told us many interesting stories about this place, the famous Klondike region, in 1898 when he first arrived. Great treasures were being taken from rich mines by bewhiskered, mud-covered miners who ate coarse, ill-cooked food, toiled long, hard hours and sometimes threw away hard-earned pay dirt on reckless, drunken carousals. Whiskey flowed freely in the many saloons and dance halls, and some bartenders gained many a pokeful of gold dust from the sawdust sweepings from the rough floors.

One of Uncle Alf's "stateside" friends, lacking any other means to make a living, was tending bar in a saloon when he overheard a scrap of conversation about a new strike nearby. Not even stopping to remove his apron, he slipped out of the back door and headed quickly for his cabin. After hurriedly getting his coat and heavy shoes on, he ran as fast as his stubby legs could carry him to stake a claim on what proved to be one of the richest fields in that area. That man was Clarence Berry, who later became a millionaire through his mines and other properties.

Here, too, in this decaying town, the beautiful and fascinating Klondike Kate had danced and sung her way into the lives and pocketbooks of the homesick, woman-hungry miners. She knew adulation, riches, and then heartbreak when she fell in love with a young man who, mainly through her wealth, became a theater chain magnate in southern California and who later threw her over for newer loves.[8]

We heard about the perilous winter when ill-equipped gold seekers continued to pour into Dawson, causing an acute food shortage. Idle, often hungry men stole provisions from the more provident. Tempers flared, shootings occurred, and things were worsening daily when the Canadian police "mounties" stepped in. They sent a boatload of dance hall girls and unemployed men down the fast-closing river. At Circle City the river froze solid, and the hapless passengers were forced on the mercy of the reluctant townspeople for the winter.

As we left Dawson, little did we dream that in thirty years, a war, airplanes, and new roads would shake the apathetic little town and bring it back to a living, breathing entity again. In 1909, we felt a bit of sadness at its faded glory as we pushed our boats into the river and went on our way.

One sunny day when we were leisurely drifting along, Sam paddled his boat alongside ours and shouted, "We need a drag sail."

"What in the heck is a drag sail?" Uncle Ned yelled.

"When we stop for lunch, stop near some good-sized trees and I'll show you!" he answered.

Near noon we saw an unusually fine stand of conifers and pulled into shore. After lunch, some of the fellows felled a tall, slim tree and trimmed off all of the laterals while others ripped a long piece of canvas from one of the tarpaulins. This canvas was nailed to the tree pole in a long, narrow, tube-like fold. Into this long, empty pocket the men pushed a few three- or four-pound rocks, distributing them evenly. The pole was then carried down to the boats that had been maneuvered into a three abreast formation. The pole was fastened across the boats, the rock-laden fold dragging in the water. It took some doing, and Sam took his share of razzing before we got the "flotilla" into the current. But when we were all straightened out with only two rowers, one on either side, the extra weight of the drag sail helped to carry us along faster.

In places the river was narrow, and it seemed one could almost reach out and touch the tapestry of a spruce forest. In other locations the water stretched out widely with many little islands separating the current. By keeping to the main channel, we could make better time than by taking a side one that looked to be a shortcut.

Every project on our camping trip that involved a major effort was pinpointed by a celebration. On this afternoon we honored the success of our drag sail by making a batch of fudge—my project—while the coffee heated.

The days were warm, as were most of the rains that sometimes caught us on the water. On sunny days we found our flotilla allowed an occasional game of cards. These games we played in progression, changing places carefully so that all might share. The losers' penalties were usually the winners' share of camp chores. One early evening the chosen campsite was along a small tributary to the Yukon. We discovered it was swarming with whitefish, jumping and fighting their way up the small river to spawn. Uncle Ned, Woods, and Bill put on rubber boots, armed themselves with short, stout clubs, and waded into the icy water to get some fresh fish for supper. I got as close as my long, dragging skirts would allow and passed the stunned, slippery fish up to the others on the bank. The four of us got soaking wet, and Uncle Ned hit his knee on a rock in the melee. Some years later he made a trip to Mayo Brothers for surgery just because we had whitefish for supper that evening on the Yukon.

Before leaving Whitehorse on a river trip, each of us had been required to register with the Mounted Police: description, age, sex, and destination. The need for this precaution had been brought about in earlier years by the disappearance of unwanted traveling companions along the rather desolate river. Accidents had become too frequent to be plausible.

Later we came to the International Line, where American territory began, and we would have to reregister to check out of Canadian territory. The log Custom House, perched on a high riverbank, came into view and we lifted our drag sail to pull into the boat landing.

In spite of the tale I had been told, that the International Line was a golden rope, it proved instead to be a narrow path cut through the forest. It could be seen for a short way and then disappeared into the distance.

The Canadian flag waved proudly from its tall standard. Several of our men walked up to the building while the rest of us stayed in our places in the boats. The Custom House was open and the registry open on a table, but no one was in sight either in the building or around it. Dutifully, our men signed for us all, left our Whitehorse official papers, and came back to our boats.

As we got out into the river again and let down our drag sail, someone happened to look back at the checking station and saw two policemen watching us through binoculars. Soon they ran down to the landing, jumped into a canoe, and paddled quickly after us. We watched curiously as they circled around us. The second time around, Auntie whispered excitedly, "It's the drag sail. They think we are smuggling something." Evidently they had never seen one, and they finally had to ask us what we had in it. When we chorused, "Rocks!" the mounties glared and, in spite of our assurance that we had left both descriptions and registry at their office, they produced notebooks and took the information down again. When we were giving our personal descriptions, Clark said absently that he was nine feet, five inches. He looked puzzled when we all burst out laughing.

One day we left Miss Geer at a little settlement from where she would go to another one inland. She was met by a man who seemed to be a stranger. He said he had been sent by Al. Who Al was, we never knew. Nor why, or where. None of us ever saw or heard from her again.[9]

The days went languidly by. I could scarcely believe the sun could be so warm with so much ice still along the riverbanks. We stopped for a day, when necessary, to catch up on our laundry and stopped to pitch our tents if it rained too hard.

The rock formations were increasingly interesting, bringing into good use my interrupted high school course in physical geography. Little does one realize how much even a small bit of knowledge intensifies the enjoyment of our Earth's structure. At one place some picturesque rock abutments on high cliffs facing each other across the dark river were called "The Old Man" and "The Old Woman"! It is doubtful if any map would designate them so.

Another place where the river made a rather sharp turn to the west, we passed along the foot of a sheer, rocky cliff. It carried almost as much color as a patchwork quilt and was aptly called "Calico Bluff."

As the days grew longer, the bird population increased; we could hear them calling—some far overhead, others flying in flocks along the river. We wondered if the plentiful swallows were those same ones who had wintered in Capistrano Mission in faraway southern California. Then there came into our tranquil days a hint of excitement and expectation, for we would soon reach our destination, Circle City.

Three wonderful weeks had gone by since we left Whitehorse. There had been no serious accidents nor unpleasant incidents. No harsh words had been spoken—a rather remarkable achievement, we thought. We had never grown tired of sourdough hot cakes with maple syrup, or even twenty-one pots of pink beans and sowbelly! Even Woods had come to relish the sourdough!

There had been occasional bakings of corn bread served with huge ham slices. Hobo stew was another delicacy—made of bacon bits, potatoes, and onions cooked to a tasty conclusion. Chipped beef creamed with canned milk poured over mounds of snowy potatoes or hot biscuits didn't go badly when evening came.

Our versatile cooks also came up with some delicious dried fruit pies. These were scarce celebration delicacies, as two large ones were required for a sitting and our little stove would cook them only one at a time. In the making of these pies, a bottle provided a good rolling pin and a dish towel pinned tightly over our little ironing board made an adequate dough board. The fire tender who saw to the baking was never allowed to leave his post "under threat of death." Burned edges were just not tolerated. It is hard to achieve that happy medium between the heat of a roaring furnace and dying coals in a wood-burning stove.

The little ice cream freezer had turned out many gallons of vanilla ice cream. All could not agree on any other flavor!

One favorite pastime of all at our camping sites had been practice shooting—long bore rifle, pistol, or twenty-two rifles. It was soon evident that both uncles were expert marksmen, and it was a small wonder that every available place in the boat had been stored with boxes of shells. They replaced the diminishing supply at Dawson and at a settlement where the Hootalinka River poured into the Yukon. It is easy to see that people, relying on their shooting eye for a supply of fresh meat, need practice. I was trying hard to improve my score, but Uncle Alf was far from satisfied with my progress and urged me to practice more.

Came at last, then, that eventful day when navigating a bend in the river, we found ourselves facing Circle City.

Chapter 4

CIRCLE CITY TO MASTODON CREEK

CIRCLE City! All of the way down the river my companions had talked of their big city! "The biggest log cabin city in the world," they said. This was it? The name "Circle" came from the fact that the Arctic Circle was not far north. "City" was truly a misnomer[10] for the small number of log cabins scattered haphazardly about. These five or six dozen cabins bore no resemblance whatever to any city I had ever seen. Two large two-story log buildings dominated the small pier on the waterfront.

"Northern Commercial" stood out blackly on a white sign fastened above narrow windows on the upper level of the nearest building. One could walk off the pier and directly into the open door of this, the town store. Its nearness to the river facilitated the unloading of the supplies from the small steamers and stern-wheelers. These would begin their summer run after Lake Laberge had thawed and the Yukon channel was open. The other large building was the hotel and bar. Some distance back from the riverfront, a wireless tower thrust its steel skeleton high into the summer sky. It overlooked the tallest building and surrounding country.

By the time our three boats were securely moored, most of the townspeople had gathered to greet us. I was surprised to see Indian children, for no one had spoken of their settlement at the south end of town. They stood in a little group of a dozen or more of varying sizes and stared solemnly at our reception. Lean, hungry-looking dogs of a breed strange to me hung cautiously on the outskirts of the small crowd. They seemed to expect the kicks and sharp commands they got.

There were hearty greetings, back-slappings, name-callings, introductions, and general confusion. We were the first party of the season to come in from the "Outside"—a welcome diversion to these people after the long winter.

Auntie, Uncle Ned, and I went up to the hotel to get rooms for us all, leaving Uncle Alf to the unscrambling of our baggage and equipment. We had accomplished some of this when breaking up the previous night's camp. Uncle Neddie was soon back to help, and before long, each one had his own belongings in a heap and was arranging his personal plans.

Our family had already received an invitation for dinner from the Jewetts that night, but the gang would meet later in the hotel for a final goodbye. The following day, each would go his own way, except in our case and that of Andy, who would go with Woods, his uncle. Some owned mines; others had good jobs of one kind or another waiting for them. Rass planned to go immediately to Eagle Creek, where our family would join him in September.

It was characteristic of Auntie that our best clothes were unpacked, pressed, and donned for our dinner date that evening. Appropriate too, our dress, for the interior of the ordinary-looking log cabin belied its exterior—there were deep rugs, fine linens, and wine glasses that sparkled just as brightly as those in the Arctic Club in Seattle.[11] Fresh wildflowers on the table, good food, and pleasant conversation all combined to make it a real occasion.

Our hostess had a word she used repeatedly. About the third time of usage Uncle Ned had a twinkle in his eye, and going back to the hotel later, he chuckled, "Peggy, isn't this bright light 'excruciating'!" It was June and it would soon be time for the midnight sun. Even though our watches said eleven o'clock, it could easily have been afternoon. Our gang was waiting impatiently for our return and we settled down to talk until early morning. Each seemed reluctant to be the first to leave. All knew it was the end to a fine experience and would be another memory to tuck away. My family had new plans since this last trip Outside. They had sold their mine on Eagle Creek, seventy miles from Circle, to Clarence Berry, one of the lucky ones from Dawson days who was fast becoming a millionaire. Uncle Ned planned to take over mining operations for Mr. Berry the following summer on Eagle, but would do some building for him there during the winter. For this present summer, he was to go out to Miller Creek to the Berry and Lamb mines to do hydraulic work. Auntie and I were to stay in Circle until autumn, when we would all go over to Eagle Creek to live. Uncle Alf would wait in Circle for his dispensation (release) for his game warden job.

Before Uncle Ned left for Miller Creek, he and Uncle Alf rented a comfortable log cabin for us. After he left, Auntie and I would have two months to rest and relax, catch up on letters, and explore the town. Auntie looked forward to this too, because when they passed through from their Eagle Creek claims to go Outside or return, their stopover in the tiny town had been brief.

We were very comfortable in our cozy dwelling. It was surprising how many little things Auntie dug out of her luggage to make the place personal and cheerful. A natural-born homemaker, she had the rare gift of charming order without constant puttering. After getting settled, we soon dispatched letters to dear ones "Outside," and we were ready to look around a bit. Fair days and fine rains had brought out an abundance of wildflowers until they were blooming prettily all around the outskirts of town. There were banks of fireweed, Iceland poppies, wild penstemon, and many varieties strange to me.

It was fun to loiter in the big store. The fur storage room was a special attraction. It was interesting, too, to see the Indian women come in to shop for needles or a length of bright-colored cloth. Auntie and I went down to their village where we could see them at work. Their beadwork was interesting, and one of the women consented (for five dollars) to stamp on moose skin the duplicate of the beautiful pattern of blue berries and wild-flowers that she was beading on a jacket. Needles were available at the store as well as strings of colored beads. There were long needles on which to string the beads, and short ones with which to fasten the strand between every two or three beads. One characteristic prominent in the Indian color schemes was that of making all flower stems of white beads. The majority of their patterns were of flowers and leaf shapes, although there were some with birds or animals.

As soon as my bead project was well started, it was put away for winter handwork. There were too many more interesting things to do with the long days.

Auntie made some black sateen curtains (like wartime black-out curtains) to hang over the white ones for sleeping, but I sat up almost every night until two or three o'clock the next morning, playing solitaire or reading. Who wanted to sleep when it was daylight!

Before the mosquito season opened, we took many walks along the riverbank in the evenings. It was while on one of these jaunts that we had the privilege of seeing a most picturesque and moving life picture. Our attention was attracted by a strange sound of men singing, and we saw several birchbark canoes coming into land near the Indian village. The slender craft came in, in close formation abreast, and just far enough apart to allow each Indian paddler to dip his paddle first on one side, then the other, keeping in line. The men sang a throaty chant in rhythm with the strokes. As they came closer we could see the loads of fresh game and realized they were hunters returning after a successful day's work.

We hurried down to the landing to watch the homecoming. Their women had been on the lookout and came down quickly from the bank. The children and ever-present dogs ran around excitedly. As soon as the canoes came into shore, the hunters stepped out and strode off to the village, while the women carried the heavy carcasses and huge baskets of fish to their homes.

I also watched the tanning of some of these hides; the women, as usual, did all of the work. They scraped them for hours with a sharp, bladed stone. At a later stage in the process a structure of branches was set up and a hide stretched securely around it. A small fire was kept smoldering on the ground beneath. Finally, the hide became a lovely golden brown or russet shade. When at last all necessary operations of the tedious process were at an end, the pelt was soft and pliable, ready to be made into moccasins, jackets, mittens, or other useful garments.

Auntie bought a lovely pair of beaded gauntlet mittens with moccasins to match for me. They were lined with red woolen blanket material, with a band of otter fur at the wrist and another wider band of the same fur at the top of the gauntlet. These were made of moose hide, as were the moccasins that matched both in beadwork pattern and a wide band of fur at the ankles. Both of these articles of clothing were ideal for winter wear, since the temperature here in winter was often thirty or forty degrees below zero. Old-timers reported a low of seventy-five below during one frigid winter.

Auntie and I met and visited the other women in Circle: the storekeeper's wife, the postmistress, and one of the owners of the small hand laundry. It was a strange feeling to learn that I was the only white girl within 200 miles.[12]

We went to see the family of the Danish teamster Nels Rasmussen,[13] who hauled supplies out to the camps and road-houses. He was a good friend of the family. He had a sweet, part-Indian wife and four good-looking children. One little girl was a beauty, and her childish face surrounded by a fur parka was caught by an enterprising photographer. Her picture, printed on postcards, netted him $1,000 at the Alaska Yukon Pacific Exposition that summer.

Mrs. Rasmussen's sister, Helen Callahan, a most attractive girl of twenty, was visiting from Fairbanks and the two of us spent many happy hours together.[14] It was pleasant to have about someone near my own age, and Auntie was spared my avid curiosity that took me everywhere. My new companion watched with me through the night of June 21 the wondrous panorama of the midnight sun, though it was old stuff to her. On that night as midnight approached, the sun came down almost to the horizon, slid along a short way and arched upward again. Its shining path made a golden necklace that seemed to encircle a section of the sky and was then pulled slowly up into its regular path.

One evening after a bit of my teasing her, Helen piloted me out to the little Indian cemetery, though she was hard put to understand why that place could be of interest. The little house built over each grave was typical of those northern tribes. Some strings of beads and trinkets hung on sections of low picket fence that surrounded some of the graves. We are told that in centuries past the dead were hung in trees, but that must have been long ago.

All at once, as if the Indian spirits were guarding their dead, we were encircled and attacked by a greedy swarm of mosquitoes. We ran almost every step of the way back to town, fighting the swirling, enveloping beasties.

Now, only one thing remained for me to do to become a "sourdough." On entering Alaska, I was called a "cheechako" and told that to become a real sourdough, I must see the breakup of the Yukon, shake hands with a later-arriving cheechako, see the midnight sun, be bitten by an Alaska mosquito, and pick up a nugget from a mine.

Our exploration led us to the opera house on the street behind the waterfront. When Circle had been in its heyday a few years earlier, the big log cabin had been full to bursting. Traveling troops of dancing girls brought to life the rough board stage, liquor flowed freely, and gold dust was the exchange for songs, drinks, and a few hours of entertainment for the miners. The building stood vacant now and was seldom used except for an occasional dance or a Christmas party.[15]

Some of the log cabins around the town had roof extensions jutting straight out over the front entrances. It gave them a ludicrous aspect, looking as if they wore slat sunbonnets.

On the Fourth of July, many of the miners came in from the surrounding creeks, and everyone donned his very best Sunday clothes. American flags flew from almost every building, and the big N.C. flew a beautiful silk one. These patriotic reminders gladdened the hearts of all and made these remote citizens realize anew that they were still a part of our nation.

There was a big, flat raft moored at the pier and in the afternoon it was filled to standing room only. It was fun to get on the river again, even though for only a short ride. The highlight of the day came when a lucky shot from the riverbank set off a charge of dynamite planted on one of the little islands in the river across from the town. This was a "men only" contest, and there was the usual betting on the result. There was constant gambling on every little event in Circle, and it was surprising how large the stakes were for the sketchiest contest.

The river steamers were now coming in regularly, and they always gave us voluble notice by several blasts on their shrill whistles long before arriving at the small pier. By the time the gangplank was down, everyone in town who could manage to be free hurried out to be on hand. Even if there were no passengers, there were always supplies and mail. As the ship's crew pushed the iron dollies piled high with mail bags and freight, they stared and smiled at us while going on with their work. Almost as soon as the mail bags hit the ground, they were snatched up and carried in a run to the post office. Eager faces appeared at the little delivery wicket long before the busy postmistress had time to sort all the mail.

Like any other small town, Circle had small bits of gossip breathing around. It was reported that Old Man Reed had advertised in an Outside paper for a wife! Imagine! And him past sixty! Mr. Reed had a small fix-it shop, and for some reason many people thought he was a wealthy man. He had no family except a ne'er-do-well son in Seattle with whom he had no contact. Each mail that arrived brought curious glances and comments about the Reed mail. "Did he get a letter?" "Yes, two. One looked like an advertisement for cough syrup." Nothing came of this during our stay in the little town, but the affair that grew out of the lonely old man's search for romance had a tragic ending the following winter.

There were four young soldiers posted at the wireless station. Two at a time, they came to call occasionally. Three of them seemed to enjoy the tea and an opportunity to talk about their families. All were admittedly homesick, but the last one was anti-everything—almost to the point of rudeness. It was not surprising that his bad manners with the Indians brought him almost to disaster. At potlatch time, their village was all astir at the prospect of their annual celebration. As was customary, four of the strong men went around the town carrying a blanket outstretched, one holding firmly on each corner. They solicited food, candy, or anything else that would add to their feast. Those lacking commodities could toss coins instead. The surly soldier refused to donate in a very insulting manner, and though he ran to hide in one of their houses, the Indians followed, caught him, and threw him in the blanket (after carefully emptying it of the treasured collection gifts). Grasping a firm handful of the tough blanket corners, they tossed him up with the blanket. Higher and higher he was bumped upward until his head was dangerously near the ceiling rafters. Finally, realizing his predicament, he begged for mercy and yelled promises.

One day in July, Auntie and I had a visitor—an old friend of the family, Chris Harrington, who owned a mine on Mastodon Creek.[16] On the surface it was just a friendly visit, but before long he blurted out, "Mrs. Garner, my cook quit, and I'm in a jam. Won't you and your niece please come out and cook for me until I can get another one?"

Auntie laughed at him and said, "Chris, you know good and well that if we went out there you'd never even try to find another cook. Besides, you know I am not supposed to do very much for a while. I don't know what Ned would say."[17]

He brightened, "I talked to Ned before I came."

"Maybe you did," she countered, "but you know, and I know, that he made you no promises."

"No, he didn't," he admitted, "but he said you knew what you wanted to do, and felt like doing, better than he did. I would pay you well and I would sure try to get another cook."

Auntie concluded the conversation by saying, "You go on, Chris, and do your errands, and Peggy and I will talk it over."

After a month in the narrow confines of Circle, I found anything that would provide new sights and experiences appealed to me. My opinion was favorable. Auntie reminded me that it would be hard work, but that was small deterrent. What finally decided the question, perhaps, was that Uncle Ned would be nearer and could be with us more often. Things were a bit flat now that Uncle Alf was gone, too. We would go.

When Chris returned somewhat fearfully for his answer, I thought for a minute he was going to cry when Auntie said we had decided to go—until he got another cook. She gave him a note to deliver to Uncle Ned, asking him to come for us on the weekend.

The next days we were busy sorting and packing our belongings for storage to be taken to Eagle Creek later. When Uncle Neddie came on Saturday, we had all loose ends tied and I, at least, was eager for the change. We were all dressed up, in spite of the fact we were going farther into the wilderness—hats, gloves, and umbrella to shield our complexions from the July sun!

Chapter 5

HARRINGTON'S MINE

I**T** was mid-July when Uncle Ed came to take us out to Chris's mine. He drove a team of bay horses hitched to a buckboard, and when we left Circle, a small mule was tied on behind to be left along the way.

We had packed and stored most of our things, taking with us only our work clothes and one dress-up outfit each. Aunt Nellie said, "You just never know!" Uncle Ed chuckled, "No, you just don't!"

The road was fairly good except for a few stretches of tundra tussock swamps. In those places the road was made of small saplings laid side by side crosswise of the roadbed.

After the tales I had heard of "Old Man Stade,"[18] I was relieved that we stopped at Jump Off only long enough for a greeting. One of many rumors had it that he speared the meat he was frying with the same fork with which he absently combed his long, grey, greasy-looking beard.

We stopped briefly at Jump Off[19] to leave the mule. We had lunch at Twelve Mile House and went on to Central House where we stayed overnight with the Baylesses.[20] These three friends of the family (I must confess, everyone we met acted as if we were long-lost and much-loved relatives) were Mr. and Mrs. Bayless and Mr. Bayless's unmarried sister. The two women were avid gardeners, and all of the metal food containers from over the years were filled with blooming plants. I thought it impossible that both flowers and vegetables had grown so fast in the comparatively short time since snow had covered everything.

There were many varieties of flowers blooming along the way, and in places the vegetation encroached on the narrow roadway, brushing the sides of our horses as they passed.

Having had a full week of a detested cooking job, Chris was delighted to see us. He led us to our quarters, which were in a large tent with board floors and sides. It was very clean and later we learned that the mining crew had been put to work for a full day getting everything in order for us.

Partitions at one end of the long room provided two small bedrooms, each furnished with bed, crude dresser, and curtained area for our clothing. I was gratified to find a shelf in my compartment partially filled with books and old magazines. At the opposite end of the tent on one side was a large range with a barrel attached by means of pipes into the firebox, which provided hot water. Across from the stove was a square galvanized sink from which the water drained off down the ravine. A large barrel of cold water stood just inside the door. There was a two-tiered baking table and many shelves. Nails driven into the wall took care of the pots and pans. Plain ironstone dishware was stacked on the shelves. The work quarters were completed by a long oil-cloth covered table with an equally long bench on each side.

Since the tent was almost on the bank of the creek, we could see the mining operations a short distance away. The work was hand-done, that is, as the pay dirt was loosened by small charges of dynamite or by use of a pick, it was shoveled into the water that ran through the sluice boxes. Riffles in the bottom of these U-shaped troughs caught the heavy particles of gold dust, colors, and nuggets. At intervals, the water was diverted, the riffle sections were taken out, and the precious metal particles were collected from the bottom and sides of the sluice boxes. Then they were washed by hand in a gold pan, dried, and placed in a tin can or leather pouch called a poke.

Since there were no banks in Circle, a miner had three choices—he could send the poke to Fairbanks, put it in the

Northern Commercial Co. vault, or risk keeping it hidden at his diggings. The day after our arrival, Chris invited me down for my first sight of a gold mine. We started at the end of the chain of sluice boxes where the water first entered—past where the shoveling crew was throwing the dirt and gravel into the fast-flowing water—to the end where it ran back onto the creek. Chris explained each step of the process. Near the end of one of the riffles he invited me to dig in and retrieve a small gold nugget shining there. Finding the nugget completed all my requirements. Now I was a sourdough!

Auntie was right when she predicted that Chris would never look for another cook. However, he tried in every possible way to make everything as convenient and as easy as he could. Any available commodity that Auntie wished for, Chris got immediately, and since she was a marvelous cook, Chris and the crew smacked their lips over the tasty meals.

Because there were two of us, the work was not too hard. There was always someone dropping in to see Chris or us. Sometimes instead of nine we had as many as seventeen to cook for. Alaska hospitality, I learned, meant a full and free larder.

There was an abundance of reading matter. We had a phonograph with some red seal records, and with solitaire to play, I was never bored. It was wonderful to me to have someone with whom to share work and responsibility—most of my happily received pay tendered in love and affection. These were things that dollars could not buy, a lesson I had learned in some of my sixteen non-secure years, and I tried willingly to deserve my aunt's confidence.

Somehow I began calling Auntie "Mother," which gave me a warm feeling and seemed to please her immensely. Mother did not encourage me to leave the cookhouse alone, although I loved to hike around. There were miners from other mines around. Many of the workers were "floaters" who did shovel work in the summer months and holed up during the long winter, eating and drinking what they could buy from their hard-earned pay. Passage in and out of the gold country being costly, many of those who had used all of their savings to get into the mining country were long in accumulating enough to get out again.

One short evening walk, Mother and I found a cranberry patch not far from the mine. All of the cranberries I had read about grew in bogs, and those sold in our California markets were almost as large as small cherries. These Alaska cranberries I found were smaller by half and of a lighter red. Chris brought out a small keg and asked me to pick enough to fill it for him. As I came in with a pail full each afternoon the following week, Mother had me wash and drain the fruit, put it in the keg, and cover it with almost that much sugar. When the keg was full to the top and put in a cool place, Chris presented me with a twenty-dollar gold piece. "Cheap at the price, and well worth it," he said. To me, twenty dollars was quite a wage.

One day we heard women's voices in ribald singing and saw two of them dressed in men's clothing reeling drunkenly along the creek. "Drunk as hoot owls," Mother said and shooed me quickly inside, lest they embarrass us. "Mary must have company," Mother said sadly as she told me about poor old prostitute Mary—about the filthy way she lived and about the unspeakable orgies that went on at her cabin. Two extremes of womanhood were she and Mother. Mother could look like a miniature duchess, even while cooking for a crew of hungry miners. Small wonder Mother was admired by all who knew her, with her pretty, frilly white blouses with their lacy boned collars, neat dark skirts and spotless tiny white aprons and kindly, feminine way. At the other extreme was poor, slovenly Mary, who wore men's clothing and lived a life of debauchery. Here was a side of life of which I knew almost nothing, and I was grateful that Mother was understanding enough to explain. Nor did she object when many months later, Mary herself (though half intoxicated) told me her own pitiful story.

Chas Lamb of Berry and Lamb on Miller Creek had the first board house built there for his wife's comfort and convenience. They had roughed it before they had struck it rich in another region, and he loved to tell of the time he had satisfied her ardent wish for a broom by paying fourteen dollars for one after their strike.[21]

After our arrival on Mastodon, the Lambs had come in from Outside to spend a few weeks of the summer at their house. Mrs. Lamb got up a party and one Saturday night everyone within walking distance (or riding if they had the means—and few did) assembled for an old-fashioned "hoedown." Some of the men tied aprons around their middles and took women's places in the square dance sets. Such a mix-up! The fiddler played, boots thumped, the men whooped, and the walls seemed to shake. There was plenty of beer, sherry for the ladies, stacks of sandwiches, big pots of coffee, and plates of "store" cookies. You could make your own selection—your own capacity being the limit. Everyone seemed to keep within fun limits, however, and the party was enjoyed until three o'clock in the morning. After it was all over, I was sure thankful that we didn't have to walk home. My poor feet were killing me!

After we had been cooking about a month, a new man came in one evening for supper with the work crew. He was a huge, ugly man, dark-skinned with straight black hair. Sullen and aloof, he ate rudely and ravenously and when asked if he had come in on the steamer, he just grunted. Two days after the stranger came to work, Mother said, "Honey, when I ring the bell for meals after this, I want you to go into your room before the men come in and stay there. I don't like the way that horrible man stares at you." So for the remainder of our stay, that was our routine. We hoped and expected that when we left that would be the last we would ever see of "Gus the Goon"—our nickname for him. How wrong we were.

It was almost September, a light snow had fallen, and it was high time we were getting over to Eagle Creek. Mining operations were slowing and closing everywhere. Many of the workers and owners were expecting to catch the last boats out before the Yukon closed in for the winter.

Uncle Ed was anxious to get to Eagle Creek, for he had not one, but two log cabins to build. Versatile Sam Warren, who had come down the river with us in the spring, was going along to work on the buildings. The four of us with a pack mule set out on horseback. We took turns juggling the big phonograph horn that we had bought while at Harrington's. "A louder one than the family already had," Uncle Ed laughed.[22]

The trail was a well-used one that led over Eagle Pass, and that area looked as though Nature had used a large broom and strong winds to delete the vegetation and expose the rocky underlay. After we began to descend into the little valley on the other side, the trail tended to follow the creek, and we passed deserted cabins on Clarence Berry's property. Once hand-mining had been done here, but each of the claims would soon be worked over by strong hydraulic pressure. We passed the cabin that Uncle Alf and Uncle Ed had built and lived in, and I made a mental note to return soon and look it over. Mother's letters written during the years they had lived there had made the place doubly interesting.

It seemed the horses knew we were coming to the end of our journey—they seemed to jog along a bit faster. Mother dropped behind and slipped off her horse long enough to get a last picture. The trail led through a brushy area, the little valley widened out, and ahead of us we could see the Berry mine and our future home.

Perhaps this homecoming would not have appealed to many. To me it meant an exciting prospect, sort of a climax to the summer activities. Best of all—home!

Chapter 6

HOMECOMING—EAGLE CREEK

T HE log cabin in which we were to live until the new and larger one was built sat solidly back some distance from the creek, facing the trail that lay along the bank. Rass hurried out to greet us, his pleasant face glowing a warm welcome.

The combined kitchen-living room smelled fragrantly of freshly baked bread, and a pot of beans waited on the stove, bubbling hot. There was a deal of "catching up" on our talk, since we had not seen Rass since June, and as soon as we had eaten, we hurried outside to see the preparations for the new building.

Over the summer Rass and a helper had cut, trimmed, and hauled down from the surrounding hills a huge pile of logs.[23] A load of lumber hauled from Jump Off the previous winter for rafters, floors, and finishing was stacked neatly by. A spot just a few feet from the present cabin had been cleared and leveled. Sam, Uncle Ed, and Rass agreed there was nothing to prevent an early start on the project the next day.

Now that we were home I was given full freedom to explore wherever I wished. Mother and I mutually agreed that we would work together mornings, but after lunch until five o'clock, I would be free to do as I wished.

Knowing that I was primarily an "outdoor girl," Mother had wisely supervised the assembling of suitable clothing for both winter and summer. My khaki divided skirt and Norfolk jacket with the well-worn and beloved Sam Browne hat filled only part of my future needs. There were stout leather hiking boots, short rubber ones for use in swampy places and in thawing snow, overshoes and snowpacks, felt Juliets or house slippers to slip on in the house. There was a fur cap with flaps to pull down over my ears and material to make a winter parka. At this still mild season, long-handled woolens looked formidable, along with woolen socks. There was a mannish-looking slicker and fur mittens. The latter I found served better when worn under the moose skin, wool-lined gauntlets Mother had bought from the Indian women in Circle. Mother would not allow me to wear trousers. I wouldn't have wanted to anyway after seeing old Mary in hers—and Bermuda shorts or toreador pants had not been dreamed up then.

After I had surveyed our immediate surroundings, I set out to get acquainted with the dogs. There was wise old papa Hans, the leader who had sired the three strong young dogs, Fox, Jeff, and Lion. Fox was even-tempered and friendly. His black and white coat of stiff hair often stuck out like a ruffled-up chicken. Jeff had even shorter hair and the pattern on his black and white sides was entirely different. His disposition was much like Uncle Ned's. He was always frisking around, getting into mischief, and seemed always to be grinning. Lion, the wheel dog, was long of body, had shaggy grey hair and a surly, noncooperative attitude. It took many weeks of acquaintance with me for him to become friendly. Old black Fritz was an extra dog, but one who could be used in the team on short hauls. He was an "outside" dog, whose curly hair and large ears bespoke his breed, bird dog. Hans and Fritz were real pals. It was a strange companionship, this wise old leader whose ancestors were wolves and an acclimated stranger. As happens in malamute law, once Fritz inadvertently got on the bottom of a pile of snarling, fighting dogs and was bitten severely. After it was all over, Hans was found lying in front of Fritz, companionably licking the wounded paw. Fritz was lucky at that, for often the bottom dog is injured fatally. I was fascinated when I saw the first dog food being cooked. This was done in a deep rectangular pan made of metal, which covered almost half of the big stove's top and was first half-filled with warm water. To this were added bits of dried fish, bacon rinds, or bones and scraps of fresh caribou or moose. After the mixture cooked long enough to soften the dried components and release the juices from the bones and meat, it was thickened with a flour and water paste to which cereal had been added. Mother wrinkled her pretty nose and was happy to see the hot stuff carried out to the woodpile to cool. She hurriedly burned some spices in the long-handled fire pan and carried the pan aloft, wafting the spicy fragrance through the house.

Each of the dogs had its own dish and was trained to wait until all of their pans had been filled. They sat up stolidly with pained expressions, nostrils quivering, until the welcome signal, "Fall to, boys."

I explored the hills, gathering rock specimens and flower seed pods, floundering and splashing along the creek, and startling strange varieties of birds. Life was wonderful!

We were so busy with daily living that the days flew. The logs were notched and lifted higher and higher. It was really more like building three cabins, a large one for our dining-living area, one built on the side of this room which, partitioned, formed two bedrooms. An alcove near the big room made space for a bed on either side of a big Franklin stove. The room added on the rear of the big one was the kitchen with a door cut to the outside. This allowed for easy access to the woodpile and two caches—one for cold storage, the other a meat cache set high above the ground out of reach of stray animals.

When it was time for the log chinking, I was allowed to help gather the moss we used to fill in the cracks. The men stopped building only long enough to kill some caribou for our winter fresh meat. They went farther away to find a huge moose.

Soon the snow was deep enough to use the dog team. Mother taught me to drive.

Uncle Ed had decided to wait until after the Christmas holidays to build the second log cabin. It was to be built for Mr. and Mrs. Berry's convenience, and they were not expected until the following summer.

One night early in November before we had moved into the new cabin, Uncle Ned, Rass, Mother, and I were discussing holiday plans. Uncle Ned said, "Rass, I think we had better go over to Butte and do our assessment work. We have to do it anyway before the first of the year.[24] If we get it done now," he continued, "we can get back in time to finish the house before Thanksgiving and have less to do in December." The work he was speaking of was the annual requirement by the government to prove up on mining claims staked there by the family and Rass. A small cabin had already been built, and additional improvements and preparations for mining later were to be continued.

"Who will stay with us?" I asked curiously. Mother laughed merrily, "Why, we will be as snug as a bug here. We won't have to cook, or even get out of bed if we would rather sleep than eat. If the weather is good, you can go hiking every day as usual."[25]

"Maybe you can go with me," I said eagerly, "if you haven't anything to do."

"No, thank you," she smiled. "You do the hiking. I have a stack of unanswered letters to work on, and I want to get started on some Christmas presents. We will both go along next time when things are a bit farther along at the claims. I am glad that you are with me," she added, "for now I won't have to go along. We will be more comfortable here this time."

"How long will you be gone, Ed?" she asked.

"I think we will stay ten days," he guessed, "if the weather holds good. We will get our stuff together tomorrow and go over the day following."

At the designated time, with the sled loaded and the dogs in harness, the men drove off over the snow-covered hills and were soon lost to sight. It suddenly seemed very quiet, and I turned a bit anxiously to speak to Mother. She was already disappearing through the cabin door, humming softly, evidently quite unperturbed that now we two were entirely alone, our nearest neighbor a solitary old miner who lived two miles up the creek.

The second day after Uncle Ed went away we had a visitor—a lone hiker evidently on his way to Fairbanks. He was a short, slender man bewhiskered, and his clothes were slightly unkempt. He had a most unpleasant manner and without other greeting demanded, "Have you got any whiskey?"

Mother answered quietly, "We do not sell liquor."

"My God," he shouted angrily, "Whoever said it was ten miles from Miller House here was a damn liar! And then," he thundered, "not a damn thing to drink."

"I can get you something to eat," Mother said calmly.

"Who said I was hungry!" he asked angrily. Mother drew herself up to her full five feet two (in high heels) and asked shortly, "If you wanted a drink so badly, why didn't you bring one with you?"

"Carry whiskey over that beast of a trail? Humph, not me!"

Mother answered tartly, "Well, you didn't need to bring a barrel!"

That stopped him cold. He gave mother a queer look, jammed his cap down over his ears, picked up his knapsack and started toward Fairbanks. After a few steps, he turned back and growled, "How far is it to Fairbanks?"

"It is 130 miles and some of the stopping places will have whiskey to sell," she told him.

As we went into the kitchen, Mother fumed, "Every year more outsiders come into Alaska who act like they own the place. Many of them flat broke, too," she added.

A few days after our cranky visitor passed by, I came in late one afternoon from hunting to find a very uneasy little companion. "Peggy," she half-whispered, "Do you know who is in the bunkhouse?"

I shook my head and whispered back, sobered by the alarm in her eyes, "No, who?"

"Ugly old Gus, the goon! You know—the man that worked for Chris this summer. He stumbled in nearly exhausted a little while ago. He's asleep now—don't you hear him snoring? He wants to stay all night and go on early in the morning," she finished.

"Well, let him," I said airily. "You can shoot him if he gets fresh!"

"Be quiet!" she whispered, warningly. "Get out of your wraps and into your room. I want you to stay there while he is here. I am going to get him some supper now."

Mother set about cooking a hot supper while I washed up and disappeared into my bedroom. Before she called Gus in to eat, she pulled a heavy bench across the curtained door that led into her bedroom. (My small room was beyond—separated from hers by a blanket hung from a wire.) Then she slid some cartridges into the chamber of my .22 rifle and leaned the gun under our hunting coats out of sight.

Gus ate wolfishly and ravenously. Mother urged that he eat more meat as she refilled the platter from the frying pan on the stove.

He mumbled, "Where are your men?"

Quickly she answered, "Oh, they are hauling wood and I am expecting them any minute. That's why I fried so much meat. It is good any time." Gus ate another helping, but appeared to be getting sleepier by the minute. After a gulp of hot coffee he asked, "Where is your niece?"

"Oh, we think she has the measles," she answered soberly. He made no comment but gulped a huge bite of pie, pushed his chair back from the table, and disappeared into the bunk room.

Almost immediately we could hear his heavy snoring and decided he must have gone to sleep in his clothes, boots and all. While Mother was cleaning up and scalding the dishes, she brought me some supper but drank only a cup of coffee herself. After she had finished the kitchen work and brought in wood (my job when we were alone), she got out her pistol and loaded it. Since there was only a blanket door into the bunk room from the kitchen, she pulled a small table in front of it and placed a jar of water there. Should Gus awake and want a drink, it would not be necessary for him to enter the kitchen.

Not really realizing the possible seriousness of our isolation, nor the wisdom of protective measures, I scoffingly got the scissors and the curling iron and laid both open on the little chest by her bed. I whispered dramatically, "Did you leave a pot of boiling water on the stove?" while I put some lipstick spots on my face.

She shook her head reprovingly, but said only, "We will sleep in our clothes. Put your shoes right where you can get into them quickly. I will keep my Juliets on."

Later Mother said she never closed her eyes all night. She left her lamp burning and got to her feet every time Gus's bed gave the slightest creak.

However, the night finally passed. Mother got up early, waked me, and started getting the fire going. She had banked a bed of coals so well that it was not long before the smell of coffee swirled into my room. She sliced a large pan of ham and stirred up some sourdough for hotcakes. I was still "having measles" and reading by a candle.

When Gus came in for breakfast, he looked a bit more rested and started right off asking Mother a lot of questions, most of them about money. How much did she make last summer? How much did her niece make? She made up a sad story about all of her destitute relations "Outside"—a poor old mother and father, many poor sisters too. It took all that she earned for them and it had already been sent away. Then he asked if they hadn't sold a valuable mine. What did they do with all of that money? Mother had a ready answer for every question and finally he must have been almost convinced that we were indeed a poor outfit. I say "almost convinced" but when he finally got ready to pay for his night's lodgings, he brought out a twenty-dollar gold piece.

Mother said earnestly, "But I can't change that. I do have a gold scale, though, and I could weigh dust if you have it."

I was listening with every nerve atingle behind Mother's blanket curtain and eyeing the pistol. I had finally become uneasy at all of the questions about family finances.

Gus dug out his dust poke and poured some of it in the scales. Mother weighed it carefully and poured some of it back. With no further questions, the ugly man jammed his fur cap over his thatch of black hair and strode out of the house. He seemed nervous and distraught as he got outside and looked back down the trail toward Miller House. Then he plodded off toward Fairbanks.

Mother watched until Gus was out of sight around a turn in the trail. Then she said, "Honey, put on your wraps, take the rifle, and go up on the hill where you can see the trail. If Gus should turn back, shoot to let me know and then come back here as fast as you can."

"How exciting," I thought, as I started off. "Wouldn't Uncle Neddie laugh at us two scaredy-cats?" But Mother meant business, so I did as she ordered. I saw the tall dark figure against the snow grow smaller and smaller and finally disappear in the distance.

I turned to go back home and hurried a bit as I thought of how concerned Mother had been. I found her drinking strong, black coffee. She really looked done in, but refused to go back to bed. By lunch time she had lost her anxiety (or hid it well) and we laughed at ourselves. Before we had completely regained our composure, however, the bells of a dog team announced the approach of another visitor.

It was the marshal from Circle.

"Where's Ed?" he asked.

"He and Rass are over on Butte doing assessment. They've been gone nearly a week." Mother answered.

"You two all alone here?" the marshal asked incredulously.

"Yes," Mother nodded and asked, "Why?"

"Did a big, ugly, dark-skinned man pass by here yesterday?" he questioned.

"Yes," Mother answered, sitting out on the edge of her chair.

"He stayed all night here last night," I broke in. "You should have seen her line up her guns."

A look of shock came over his face and then he turned back to Mother. "Mrs. Garner, that man robbed a miner over near Miller Creek. He beat the man almost to death with a piece of stove wood. That thug is trying to get away. Darn fool hasn't a chance. But, good God, he might have killed you both!"

Chapter 7

MOVING IN

SOON after our men returned from doing the assessment work, we moved into the big new cabin and got out our pretties to make it home.[26] The walls in the main room were lined with green burlap, as were those in our bedrooms. Mother put fur robes and fancy pillows on the alcove beds. With the big Franklin stove between the two couches, this made a fine spot to curl up with a book. The little cuckoo who lived in the clock on the wall nearby came out faithfully to announce the hour. There were white curtains for all of the house windows, and the phonograph we had carried so carefully over the pass had its own little homemade table near a hand-done bookcase. A big, long table in our living-dining area was surely multipurpose, for it served for eating, ironing, writing letters, playing cards, and cutting out sewing projects.

The kitchen was a nice, light room with windows facing in three directions. There was a huge wood-burning range with the usual attached barrel for hot water, a zinc-covered table for bread-baking, and many shelves and hooks most convenient for our work. Wood, collected even during the building program, was cut and piled in neat, long cords close to the kitchen door.

As the snow got deeper and the trails packed, Nels Rasmussen, the teamster from Circle, brought out our winter supplies. Mother had ordered provisions in such quantity, it seemed far too much. There were cases of vanilla and spices, barrels of butter in brine, dried eggs, dried potatoes, boxes and boxes of canned fruits and vegetables, hams, huge sides of bacon, sacks of flour, bags of cornmeal, and many pounds of dried fruit. There were matches, dried yeast, sugar, salt, and molasses—enough for a small store it seemed.

The dispersal and storage of all of this mountain of stuff were no small chore. The warm storage items were hustled out of their layer of wool blankets into a shallow cellar beneath the kitchen. The hams and bacons were hung out in a small log building built for that special purpose, called a "cold cache." Canned things and staples that would freeze safely were also stored there. There was a smaller cache outside about five or six feet square, built on stilts as protection for the food from wild animals. This was equipped with hooks and racks for fresh meat and game. Here caribou and moose meat, ptarmigan, wild rabbits, or other fresh game would freeze solid, but they had to be used before summer thaw.

The mailman's weekly arrival was always exciting. It was a real event, for besides welcome letters from our dear ones Outside or packages from the mail-order houses, he brought bits of local gossip and news from other miners along his route. One piece of tragic news was that Old Man Reed's mail-order bride had arrived at Circle coincidentally on the same steamer with his ne'er-do-well son. The two young people had fallen in love and hoped, on landing, to receive the old man's forgiveness and blessing. Instead, a terrible quarrel had developed after a few days, and the son had killed his father, the woman, and then himself, ending the trouble for all three of them.

As soon as the snowpack permitted (even before the horse trail was usable), Mother and I harnessed the dogs and drove up and down the creek and over the nearest hills. Until I got the hang of driving, I rode in the sleigh while she started them with an emphatic "Mush on!" and away they went, tails wagging, bells jangling. Their harness consisted of collars, traces, and connecting straps—no driving lines of any kind. Any change of direction was given by "Gee" or "Haw," and as soon as they got into the trot, Mother jumped up on the long runners (the little extensions behind the sled) and rode standing. The dogs really seemed to enjoy their work and responded alertly to the shouted directions. Sometimes they crossed a set of fresh rabbit tracks, ran away, left the trail, and ended up in a confused tangle. Mother scolded, "Hans, you bad boy. You know better than that." Then she got them unscrambled and in order. How she loved those dogs, and her affection brought a constant response. She told me how Hans snapped at the three pups to bring them to order when they were first being trained for the team. If they didn't jump into their collars at the first command, he growled and snapped at them until they did what they were told to do.

Returning from a drive one very cold day, our dogs spied three scrawny Indian dogs running loose around our cabin. They had seen these dogs many times, as they belonged to a neighbor, Mr. Bowman,[27] who lived a mile or two down the creek. The neighbor was a grouchy old individual who often came to visit. Usually he left his dogs at home. On this occasion, some means of communication went on between Hans and his "boy"— with one accord, they leaped forward, snarling, to greet the impostors. In a jiffy, eight snapping, snarling, fighting dogs were jumbled up together, fighting furiously.

Uncle Ned was working near the cabin and had a good laugh watching Mother (all 100 pounds of her) pounding any convenient dog's rump that she could reach with her small mitted fist. However, when he realized that she could not hear his warning to "Get away, Nell," he came running to stop the fracas. A pack of malamutes fighting is a serious thing, for often the bottom dog gets killed if they are allowed to fight to the end. After the team had been unharnessed and the neighbor dogs tied, Mother went to Hans and said, "Shame on you. SHAME on you." The old fellow could not meet her eyes—he looked instead off down the creek and then put his head down on his paws.

When the new log cabin had been built alongside the old one, a narrow passage between had been left for dog kennels, thus providing a maximum of protection from the wind for them. Each dog had its own personal house with an entrance just large enough for its body and, in winter, a small piece of wool blanket to sleep on. Sometimes clean straw was added. There were several extra compartments for dogs of travelers, but when there were strange dogs, all were chained in their houses at night for protection from each other.

One project, enjoyable the length of the winter, was ice cream making. Dried eggs were soaked in water, then beaten well. To these, partially diluted canned cream, flavoring, and a dash of salt were added. This mixture was poured into a small tin dishpan. Armed with the pan, a big, long-handled spoon in my hand, and protected from the cold by winter garb, I ran out to place the pan on the low roof of a kennel. Pushing and circling the warm pan in the snow, it soon made a safe, smooth landing. Then spoonfuls of white snow fluff scraped out from under the top crust were added to the mix in the pan, which I stirred well before hurrying in out of the intense cold. In a few minutes it was time to go out again and madly stir the mix so it would finish with a fine grain. The trick was to get it just right, neither too hard nor too mushy. Oh, was it good! We could have a blueberry, pineapple, or chocolate sundae.

Winter cooking was a breeze. Rass loved to bake bread, so he took over that chore. Besides the baking, he washed the supper dishes. If the weather was too cold to work outside or if there were no other duties inside, he washed all of the day's dishes. He said he liked to keep his ladies' hands white, but he really seemed to enjoy it. He sang lustily, Danish songs we could never understand, sometimes repeating one chorus endlessly.

Uncle Alf came home frequently. We had many callers, and occasionally an interesting traveler would stop for the night on his way between Circle and Fairbanks.

We played endless games of cards during the long evenings. The phonograph provided music for impromptu dancing—though this often proved a workout for Mother and me. Four or five dance-hungry men could wear a gal down!

Our home must have seemed like a palace to our lonely masculine visitors who came to call. Most of the miners lived alone and did their own cooking, cleaning, and laundry. Too many of them ate almost "from the pot," seldom used a broom, and wore the same clothing too long. Let me hasten to add, however, that there were many men who were as neat and clean as any woman.

In our home, regardless of the long days, a routine was followed religiously. There was much to be done; everyone shared and seemed to enjoy every minute of the doing. In the winter the men helped with the ironing, cooking, or whatever needed to be done, for outside of the assessment work and light chores, there was not a regular eight-hour day of the usual work. When stove wood was split from the great pile of lengths by the back door, it had only to be carried a few steps into the cabin. Hauling water in barrels on the horse-sled was not work but a lark, for the beautiful white rabbits and few twittering birds left interesting tracks, if they were not able to get out of sight before we passed. In short, as long as there was work to do, all shared, and when it was done all played and relaxed. We played cards, read, played the phonograph, or wrote letters.

One winter chore I dreaded was a letter to our physical geography class in high school. My teacher had asked, as a special favor, that I write the details of our trip inside, telling in particular about the rock formations along the Yukon. Mother hounded me until, at last, a thirty-page letter made a fat bulge in its long envelope, and I breathed a long sigh of relief.

My incessant practice with the .22 rifle eventually began to bring results, but it was not until I brought home nine ptarmigan, all shot in the head, that a compliment from Uncle Alf was forthcoming.

It was fun to prepare Thanksgiving dinner. We had ptarmigan, ham, and some kind of a substitute for the goodies we usually had Outside. Mother had made caribou mincemeat and fruitcake. I made fancy candies. When she told me she would make pickled peaches, I was skeptical, as there were only canned ones and dried ones. First, she sorted out the very nicest dried ones and poured boiling water over them. As soon as the water had cooled, the skins peeled off nicely. Matching halves of equal size, she fastened them together with toothpicks, stuck a few whole cloves in each, and dropped them into boiling spiced syrup.

In late summer, Rass had managed to pick some blueberries and put them down in sugar. These made delicious short cakes. Whipped canned milk, well-flavored, proved a very good substitute for fresh cream.

The very best linen, china, and glassware made festive our long, homemade table, and we all dressed up as though we were really going somewhere.

One cold night when Uncle Neddy went outdoors for wood he called insistently, "Peggy, Peggy. Wrap up and come out here quick."

Knowing that these summonses always meant something interesting or adventurous, I hurried to do his bidding. The sky was ablaze with a magnificent display of the northern lights. It was an awesome spectacle of brilliant color. There was orange, yellow, green, red, soft rose, violet, and blue. A scintillating banner made up of millions of pendulous prisms glimmered and glowed across the firmament. The movement of the color pattern was vertical, while intermittently a ripple, like that on the surface of a placid lake, pirouetted across the flaming streamers. Then all of the shades of the luminous vapor changed to other tints and hues of the original ones.

There was a strange noise that could be heard plainly in the night. It was unlike thunder on an autumn day, rather like the sound of a deep G note played by an orchestra made up of drums only. It was throbbing, compelling, quiet, but insistent.

Suddenly, the color pattern rearranged itself, making a variegated pattern of dazzling brilliance flung in a jagged line across the heavens. This was a fascinating and eerie apparition of magic splendor, indeed an unforgettable experience.

We knew that when these displays occurred, unheralded and erratic in timing, we were seeing one of Nature's mysterious and little-understood phenomena, a gift, so to speak, given only to those who lived in northern latitudes. We were living just outside of the Arctic Circle, and the rich gift was ours to share.

Chapter 8

CHRISTMAS HOUSE PARTY

THE snowdrifts piled higher and higher while gusty winds swirled odd, rhythmic patterns over their crests. The temperature went down to twenty and thirty degrees below zero, and as the daylight hours grew shorter, we moved in a gray world when we were out-of-doors.

It was December, and at last, the mysterious packages from the mail-order houses were opened. To my surprise and delight, they contained all of the necessary materials for Christmas decorations. Besides the many bolts of tinseled cord and shiny tree ornaments, there were numerous packages of colorful crepe paper for making artificial flowers. There were deep, rich reds and pure white for roses and carnations, green for leaves and stems, fine wire, paste, and finally, some folds of lovely blue paper for making heavenly blue morning glories.

During the long evenings and on into the night sometimes, we made literally dozens of carnations and roses and fashioned long garlands of morning glories to twine around our bedroom windows. This flower-making was something I had never done and was great fun. As we worked, I learned that Mother had been planning since June for a big Christmas house party, so I would not miss too much the family day at home with Grandma and all of the other dear ones.

Practically all of the local and Circle friends within easy traveling distance had already been invited to the "Garner House Party," and it was time for the five of us to begin making preparations for a two-day stay of at least thirty guests.

Uncle Alf came home before the holidays and made it his task to see that the tall meat cache was filled to capacity. He dressed warmly with his parka over all and went out into the white world to hunt, often taking the dog team and ranging the farther hills and valleys. Soon, long rows of plump dressed ptarmigan on narrow boards joined frozen carcasses of caribou and a huge moose in the cache. Uncle Alf brought two large turkeys and a fifteen-pound suckling pig from cold storage in Fairbanks. Finally, there was barely enough room in the cache to stand beside the table where the meat was sawed or chopped into cuts of various kinds and sizes.

While Uncle Alf hunted, Uncle Ned and Rass completed many carpentry projects inside the cabin, making new cabinets, adding convenient shelves, and building two long tables with benches for each. The latter they stored outside. As the days passed, Uncle Alf went on with this work while Rass and Mother got busy with extra baking. They made loaves and loaves of bread, long white loaves and round ones of rye. After all of the bread was wrapped and stored in the main food cache behind the cabin, the baking pans were filled with cakes, both chocolate and white. The same type of dried apples that we had soaked and stewed for pies were used to make delicious applesauce cakes, well-studded with plumped raisins. And pies!—it seemed they were countless. There were raisin, mince (caribou makes fine mincemeat), dried apples, and canned pumpkin. If the two busy cooks got more pies ready for baking at one time than the big range oven would accommodate, Uncle Ned carried them to the smaller oven in the other cabin (now called the bunkhouse) and baked them there. As he worked at keeping the oven heat constant, he simmered a large ham on the top of the stove and on following baking days, cooked two others. The three of these were later brown-sugar glazed and clove-studded to provide tasty cold cuts, along with thin slices of caribou roast.

Rass made many batches of doughnuts and as they raised to fat puffiness, I fried them in bubbling fat and rolled them in sugar. When we had finished with doughnuts, we had a fifty-pound flour sack full of them. I had never seen so much food cooked for one party, and I dashed here and there, helping with the different cooking operations, cracking nuts, making frosting, and brewing pails of hot coffee that we drank as we worked. Uncle Ned called me the "Christmas flunky," and we joked and sang as the happy days marched by. Our faces were often reddened from the heat of the big stove, but we got blasts of fresh air when it was time to replenish the wood box. No one said, "Gee, it's cold outside," when reentering the cabin but, "Gee, it smells good in here."

Several days before Christmas our stores of food were complete, the big cabin shiny clean from one end to the other, fresh curtains hung, and our decorations and flowers, save those for our tables, in place. The tiny tree that we had dug out of the snow twinkled with ornaments from the top of the bookcase where it would stay until the "big dinner," when it would center our table grouping. How beautiful it all looked!

There was time then for extra grooming and relaxing. Everything looked so festive. We were very gay and kept the phonograph playing our records of Christmas carols.

On the twenty-fourth of December we arose early and got all of the last-minute duties out of the way. By this time we had learned that we were to have eight women guests and probably more than thirty men. It was necessary to plan beds for all. Three women would sleep in each of our two bedrooms, two in one of the alcove beds, and Mother and I in the other. The men would have the bunkhouse to themselves, each of them bringing his own bedroll and finding a place for it there—whether he ever used it or not!

Early in the afternoon our guests began arriving, some "mushing" in on foot, others with dog teams and sleds. There was a great hello-ing and jingling of sleigh bells as Nels Rasmussen pulled his horses to a stop by our front entrance with a hearty "WHOA!" Nels had started from Circle with some vacant seats in the sleigh, but he had picked up friends along the way until the big freighter was filled with gay, chattering people. It was hard to tell who was who until the layers of fur robes, parkas, fur coats, and ear-flapped caps had been removed.

By supper time there were thirty-five new faces around our two long tables. Mother and Rass had made literally gallons of hearty mulligatawny soup, well-flavored with good old dried onions, using moose meat stock. This was supplemented by platters of cold meats, bread, pickles, pie, and coffee.

After supper Uncle Ned and Rass recruited a crew of willing male helpers and from then until the end of the party, Mother and I were banned from the kitchen. We were hostesses, period. If any group of women talked together long, a man said, "Break it up, girls. Give us a chance."

Mother whispered to me, "Try and talk to every man here, Honey, whether he has anything to say or not. Poor dears, some of them live alone and get so hungry to see a woman's face."

"But I am not a woman," I teased.

"You'll do," she laughed.

As soon as the dishes and food were out of the way and the tables carried out, the floor was swept and reswept and sprinkled well with Borax. It was not as smooth as a ballroom floor, but who cared?

The women all brought evening clothes, and one by one they began making "entrances" from the bedrooms. As each one emerged, smiling sweetly, cheers went up for all—then a rush by the men for a dance. Mrs. Dodson, the postmistress from Circle, was beautiful in her black lace dress and was as gay and charming as the younger women. She was seventy years young.[28]

The faithful phonograph sent out its waltzing, two-stepping melodies, and we danced and danced. At intervals someone called for a Paul Jones—soon the room echoed with "allemande left," or "Ladies in the center, all hands around—grand right and left—homeward bound." We did a Virginia reel for a rest, the three-step, and an occasional schottische. The phonograph was wound and rewound, and records changed quickly so that there was scarcely time to get one's breath between dances. The sturdy cabin seemed to pulsate as the dance went on, and we renewed our strength by quick trips to the kitchen for coffee, hot chocolate, or a piece of cake.

An alert guest with watch in hand shouted, "Merry Christmas! Merry Christmas, Merry Christmas." It echoed and re-echoed around the crowded room. Then a strange thing happened. All of our men guests stampeded out of the room and out of the cabin. Some went out of the front door and others out the back. We looked at each other in amazement. What was this all about? In a few minutes they were back, all carrying packages of various sizes and shapes. Mother had specified "no presents," but each one had a gift for Mother and me. When the mass exodus for the other cabin began, the ladies had slipped into the bedroom—they said to powder their noses—but they came back into the big room when the men began to pour in, their eyes twinkling. Each was carrying a gaily wrapped package.

Pete Anderson was pressed (pushed might be a better word) to make a presentation speech. His words were so flowery at first that one of the men shouted,[29] "Bet you read that in a book!"

Another answered, "Aw, Barney, you know he can't read!"

Pete's face got a little red, then he said a few simple words of appreciation to our family for the "swell party." He tried to express what it meant to those like himself who lived alone, to have these hours of fellowship and fun in such a nice home— "with women." He finished to great applause.

Mother made a little speech in reply, thanking each one for coming through the snow and cold to make our Christmas such a happy one. Most of the guests had a few words to say, if only a hearty "Thank you, Garners." I was surprised to see a few teary eyes. Perhaps lonely hours through weeks, months, and years brought to mind "what might have been," for we all knew that some of these men had deserted their homes and families to follow the lure of gold. Others had not intended desertion, but having failed in their search, stayed on, never quite accumulating enough to recoup the loss of the grubstake with even a few hundred dollars extra.

I was not allowed to open my packages even piecemeal. "You can do that next week," they urged, and the dance resumed. The kitchen crew kept cups and plates washed and took turns joining the dancers.

So it went until morning—no one even thought of going to bed until Uncle Ned ordered, "Everyone hit the hay. My gal is about to wear out a pair of new shoes and I can't have that."

Later, Uncle Alf carried coffee and doughnuts to the men in the bunkhouse. Uncle Ned and Rass started the big dinner preparations. It was necessary to have it early in the afternoon because some of our guests had to leave soon after that. One turkey had been roasted during the night while we danced, and the other one was joined by a huge pan of ptarmigan in the big oven. Uncle Alf waded through the maze of sleepers and card players in the bunkhouse kitchen to cook the suckling pig there.

In their quarters the women were beginning to stir sleepily, and Mother carried coffee and toast to them. The two long tables were brought in and a small one set between them—making a tall "H." The tiny, decorated tree was placed on the small table in the center. When the long, sheet-covered tables were decorated with a wealth of red crepe paper roses, red candles, and bits of conifer greens interspersed with gold tinsel, they were truly a beautiful sight, and we felt repaid for our efforts by the compliments of our admiring guests.

By the time all of the food was ready for our feast, four more male guests had arrived. The ladies were dressed "to the teeth," as Uncle Ned complimented. On Christmas Eve some of the faster-thinking men had each asked a woman to sit with him at the Christmas dinner table. The few who had wives there were not allowed to sit with them. Second-askers had the privilege of sitting on the other side of the chosen one. Mother carefully distributed these trios around both tables. She sat at the end of one long table, Uncle Ned at the other. The other table was hosted by Uncle Alf with me at the foot.

The feast, for it could be called no less, was a thing to remember and, as plates were filled and refilled, I could see how so much advance preparation had been necessary.[30]

Soon after the dinner was over, Mrs. Griffith and her sled-driver started home to Miller House, as she had much to do to prepare for many of our guests who were to be entertained there on their return trip to Circle.[31] Several others going in the same direction decided to leave also. Uncle Alf hitched our dog team and went along to see that all got safely over Eagle Pass. The wind was so violent when they reached the summit that it was necessary for Mrs. Griffith to get out of the sled and walk. In a few places steps had to be cut in the slick ice for her safety. Getting over was a slow, laborious process, but at last they surmounted the icy ridge and got safely down on the sheltered side of the pass to the trail.

Upon turning back, Uncle Alf found the home trail completely obliterated. Through the years, the pass had been swept clean of many landmarks, and erratic drifts of snow driven by cutting wind constantly changed the face of the landscape. The sleet, sharp as knives, tore at the dogs' eyes, and Uncle Alf made a quick decision. Digging a sweater out of the sled, he tied it securely around the head of Hans, the lead dog, and giving him a pat, he said, "Go on home, Boy. Mush on." Hans started out slowly until he could feel the other dogs following steadily along behind, then he increased his speed to a steady trot and came on home unerringly. The dogs' whiskers were covered with ice and their eyes rimmed with it. Uncle Alf got their harness off quickly, took them into the bunkhouse entry, and warmed them up well before taking them to their kennels.

Christmas afternoon we all rested or played cards. By eight o'clock we were ready for a snack. The "leavings," with additional bread, pastry, and coffee, were put out on our family table and each ate buffet-style, choosing according to his taste or capacity.

Once again the cabin floor was prepared for a dance—a quieter, more decorous affair than that of the previous night—and we called it quits about two o'clock. After all, there was a long trip ahead for some with more parties to anticipate along the way.

The wind went down and by morning it was cold but quiet. By noon our family was alone again, remembering the farewells—"Best party I ever went to," "God bless you," "Thank you, thank you, thank you."

When finally all of my Christmas packages were unwrapped, I was stunned. These dear people, many of whom had never seen me before, who only knew that the Garners' niece was living with them (and maybe she would stay permanently) had gone all out to give me a Merry Christmas indeed. Many of the gifts had come in from mail-order houses, from the winter stocks of the N. C. Co.[32], or overland by dog team from Fairbanks.

From my dear Alaska family there was a shining sterling silver toilet set; from Rass, an all-leather suitcase. There were many boxes of candy, mostly chocolates, and books, Indian beaded mittens, and moccasins. Many little packages revealed small gold nuggets of various shapes and sizes. These were from the hard-earned pay dirt of miners. One of the very nicest gifts of all was "Timmy," a round, fat and furry malamute puppy.

From a full heart echoed and re-echoed the party farewells—Thank you. Thank you. Thank you.

Chapter 9

At Home After Christmas

A FTER the wonderful Christmas party, guests came more often—most of them solitary miners who lived within a radius of thirty miles. Most of them owned mines of varying value or were caretakers for others. These strays would come mushing in one day, share the family hospitality, and go home the next day. Those who did not have dog teams hiked the wintry trails with only a light pack on their backs. We played cards and danced most of the night.

Besides his toilet articles and perhaps a bit of dried meat for possible emergency, the visitor invariably carried a box of somewhat stale store candy in his knapsack for "the girls," Mother and me. This candy may have been ordered weeks before when the mailman went to Fairbanks.

After some illuminating joshing by the family, I finally realized that some of these visitors came to see me. It was surely a great surprise, for to me at sixteen, any man of thirty (and practically everyone I had met was older than that) was ages older than I. To me they were simply men to treat politely, banter, play cards, or dance with. I had grown up with three older brothers, and outside of the sweetheart I had left behind in high school, no masculine admirer had caused even a tiny romantic heart throb.

The winter months went by. January, February, March came. Uncle Neddie warned, "Take all the sled rides you can, Peggy. Summer will be here before you know it."

So, after my work was done I would harness the dogs and go out over the now familiar trails. It was invigorating to run behind the sled, or, tiring, to jump on behind, the cold air pushing against the small exposed circle of my face. My parka had a band of fur around its hood and I could pull the hood tightly until only my eyes and nose were visible. On one of the coldest days I returned from a ride with a small white spot on one cheek. Immediately, the spot got a vigorous rubbing with snow while I got a scolding for staying out until my face had started to freeze.

One wintry day when there were some extra men visiting and Uncle Alf was home, they all got together and dragged a clumsy freight sled from the shed. Six of us climbed to the top of a nearby ridge, dragging the heavy thing laboriously behind us. We arranged ourselves on our stomachs as comfortably as possible and prepared to descend the icy slope. We started out slowly, gathering more and more momentum, until over a short space, we were fairly flying down toward the bottom. The combined weight of six people added to that of the long sled gave us bullet speed, and we flew faster and faster. Suddenly, Uncle Ned, who was on the front trying to steer the unwieldy sled, yelled, "Jump! A tree!" As we all rolled off one side or the other (and kept on rolling) the heavy sled crashed into a half-hidden tree stump, the front crosspiece splintered in half. Someone would surely have been seriously injured but for the timely warning. We decided regretfully that a bobsled and a freight sled were not of the same breed.

Chapter 10

CIRCLE HOT SPRINGS

AT supper one March night when Uncle Alf was at home, Uncle Ned suddenly banged the flat side of his knife on the table and said loudly, "Quiet!"

Startled, we all looked at him to see what new prank he had in mind—he was full of them.

"Let's all go camping. I need a rest!" he said impishly.

A chorus of derisive laughter greeted his proposal.

"Camping? Where? Rest?" we all asked in unison.

"All right, all right, you killjoyers. I mean it." Then drawing his mouth down, he said plaintively, "I got rheumatiz in me bones."

We hooted at that one, as he was about as active and as supple as a cat.

"Well, to be honest," he went on seriously, "I guess we don't need rest, but I would sure like to take a bath someplace where my feet didn't have to hang over while my backside soaked. Let's go over to Circle Hot Springs for a couple of weeks. We can take our stuff on the horse sled, and Nellie and Peggy can drive the dogs."

Uncle Alf chuckled, "Well, I reckon you got something there, pardner. I get a decent bath whenever I go to Fairbanks, but maybe we might see some of our Miller House friends if we took a trip over there now. No one is very busy at this season."

Looking at Mother, then at Rass, Uncle Ned asked, "How about it, Nell? Rass?" Mother showed her pretty dimples in a big smile.

"Now you know very well I'll go anywhere the rest of my family goes."

Rass nodded, "Suits me."

"No one asked me if I wanted to go," I began.

"Ha, ha!" Uncle Ned laughed. "We just knew you'd rather stay home!"

It was surprising how fast the camping idea grew into a reality. Two days later, as Uncle Alf closed the cabin doors securely (but did not lock them), Uncle Ned nailed a cardboard sign by the front one—"Gone Camping. Make yourself at Home. The Garners."[33] With Mother and me leading with the dog team, then the big sled and driver, followed by two men walking, we made a small procession. We made stops to rest the animals, to enjoy the grandeur of the snowy mountain peaks, and for lunch, but still got to the springs in the late afternoon.

A large tent and a smaller one on wood floors, each with an iron stove, were soon put up for our lodging, and we lost no time in taking advantage of the steaming baths.

The spring was covered with small, house-like structures, divided into compartments for men and women. There were separate accommodations for the native Indians who came often to bathe, as had their ancestors long before the white man came.

The bottom and sides of the bathing pools were lined with smooth boards from the lumber mill at Jump Off. More boards formed a walk on two sides of the pool where one could sit and soak tired feet.

The water was very hot and was cooled to bearable temperature by chunks of ice that had been frozen in five-gallon kerosene cans, removed from the cans, and stored in tiers in a nearby hillside.

As Uncle Ned had said, it was indeed good to have baths when one's feet didn't hang over. We bathed joyously and often, ate hearty and easily cooked food, slept late, and filled our days with simple relaxation.[34]

The word got around that the Garners were at the hot springs, and soon friends old and new came in from the creeks around to join us. Jay and Mrs. Kelly,[35] who ran a tavern at Miller House, came, and Mr. Mortensen from Deadwood[36] made our dancing more fun in the evenings. He once had been a dancing teacher. Will and George Lorenz, who were staying at the Berry and Lamb headquarters near Miller House, came over to get acquainted. They had been sent in to work on Eagle Creek when the mine there opened later.[37] Dear old Clark, one of our river trip friends, came from Mammoth Creek and Chris Harrington came from Mastodon. Pete Anderson also came over from Mastodon.[38]

What a gay, chattering crowd we were. We played ball or pitched horseshoes when the weather permitted, or played cards or danced to the music of a phonograph indoors.

Medicine Lake was nearby, and its frozen surface was perfect for dog sledding. George Lorenz and I hitched up all of the available dogs and went riding. There, too, we saw the accomplishments of a colony of beavers who lived in a tributary to the lake.

The fun-filled days tramped on one another's heels as they ran by . . . one week . . . two weeks . . . but at the end of the third week, Mother said insistently, "Boys, I just have to get home! I have some very important sewing to do."

Mother's important sewing turned out to be a new dress for my seventeenth birthday, which was coming soon. Up to this time my dress-up clothes were mostly skirts with blouses plain or frilled to suit the occasion. Besides adding some bulk to my rather pudgy figure, the blouse tails had a way of becoming disarranged—much to Mother's disapproval.

My new dress was cut in princess style, form outlining, and in the very first fitting I was overjoyed to see that my waist was thinning down a bit and that I had developed a few curves.

Hourglass figures were then the vogue, and though mine was far from that desirable state, it had improved a bit to be sure. I had a deep-seated complex about my rather pudgy figure, for the first auntie with whom I had lived for four long years had jokingly remarked, "You look like a bed tick with a string tied around the middle."

Chapter 11

ROMANCE

OTHER seemed as pleased as I when the dress with its simple, becoming lines was finished. Crowning glory— she helped put my hair up by pinning my long braids into a sort of crown around my head. She assured me that it made me look much taller and older.

Hardly had the descent from these personal clouds of glory been accomplished, when Pete Anderson came to call—ostensibly on me. His calls on our family had become more frequent since the Christmas party, but somehow this one seemed a bit different.

Contrary to the usual footwear for outdoors in winter, Pete came in wearing leather shoes! I knew that he had walked over the summit fork. Having spent most of his winters Outside, he did not own a dog team. As soon as the opportunity allowed, I asked Uncle Ned about the shoes. He laughed mischievously and whispered, "He must have stopped down the trail and put them on."

Pete was of medium height, rather squarely built, with black mustache and hair—the latter parted in a straight line without the deviation of a hair. Whatever he put on it smelled rather pleasant and surely kept his hair neat. His navy blue suit was spotless under the heavy outer clothes. I decided anew that he was not handsome but that he was pleasant and courtly with perfect manners. He had come to stay overnight, if we didn't mind, he said. This was the last time he could come, he explained, as he was making advance preparations to open his mine as soon as the thaw came.

Sometime after supper, and before anyone had an opportunity to say anything about bedtime, I went to my bedroom door, opened it, and said over my shoulder, "Well, if you will excuse me, folks, I am going to bed. I walked a long way today and I am really tired."

When Pete came in from the bunkhouse to breakfast the next morning, I had hardly said, "Good morning," when he said, "How about taking the dogs and going for a ride today, Peggy?" I looked at Mother appealingly.

"I think that would be nice," she smiled guilelessly. I looked at Uncle Ned. His face was impassive. No help there. Uncle Alf was busy eating, and Rass went out to the kitchen to get some hot biscuits.

"If Mother hasn't something I should do," I began—

"Oh, no. There is nothing," she insisted. I was trapped for sure.

"All right," I assented, "but let's wait until it gets a little warmer."

Uncle Neddie's head jerked up. He was about to say something, but checked himself in time.

I thought, "Darn traitors. They know I don't want to go riding with Pete." I went on eating.

I insisted on helping with the dishes, and Rass gave me a mischievous, understanding smile. I very carefully made my bed, smoothing every crease out of the white spread and punching the pillows to a fat puffiness. "Darn! I'd rather go riding by myself!" Smack! Smack!

About that time, Mother came bustling into my room. She hesitated for a moment, then said lightly, "Peggy, I think Pete is going to propose to you. You might tell him you are too young now, but to wait for you."[39]

I gave her one swift, incredulous glance. She meant it! She was serious! A sudden, engulfing tide of anger flashed over me, lightning-like, and I turned my eyes away lest they betray my fury. My whole body became tense and rigid. Perhaps she was embarrassed by the silence, for without another word she went out of my room and quietly closed the door.

I was glad she was gone! I had to face this unaccountable, monstrous emotion that pulsed and throbbed over my whole being. My own breath seemed to be suffocating me. Suddenly, I jerked my head around to the mirror to see if my face was as distorted as it felt. The answering image was somehow quieting. Except for a very red face and blazing eyes, it was the same face I had seen when combing my hair that morning. I breathed easier then, and a sense of composure and confidence returned as I stood quietly by the dresser trying to understand what had happened to me. Why was I so angry? I wasn't in love with Pete. Mother couldn't make me marry him. How did she know he wanted to, anyway? How dare she! I wasn't in love with anyone—or was I? What about the slight pricks of resentment over the past year when Mother had proved in many little ways that she disapproved of my Outside sweetheart?

First, there had been the matter of the small diamond ring that Earl offered as a going-away gift—"So you won't forget me," he had said.[40] When I asked dutifully if I might accept it, Mother had refused permission very definitely. It was true that he had told me he loved me on the day I was sixteen (he was seventeen) but, though we talked of a life together someday, that was for a time far in the future when our separate educations were advanced and we were older. Obediently, I had refused the ring, but I had not forgotten.

As the months with my Alaska family passed, Mother had suggested that I write more letters to my family Outside and fewer to Earl, hinting that perhaps my interest was greater than his. This had had some effect and when my letters to him had gotten fewer, he had rushed out a Special Delivery, Registered, "TO BE DELIVERED TO ADDRESSEE ONLY" letter to me. Uncle Alf had been quite stern when he returned from a trip to Circle between mails. He handed my important-looking letter to Mother, saying grimly, "It's from Earl. Think of it! Had I not been in Circle and the postmistress not known us all, Peggy would have had to make that seventy-mile trip to get it. You may give it to her, but tell her that we are going to read it, too." Uncle Ned objected mildly, but they were all a bit embarrassed when I entered the room after overhearing the conversation. This was one of the few afternoons I was not out-of-doors at that time of day.

In my letter, Earl had spoken again of his uncle who had a small candy store in Fairbanks,[41] but there was no sinister plot to elope or anything that might offend anyone. Although he had not mentioned it, I felt sure he thought my folks had been withholding his letters to me.

I handed over the letter and tried not to show the hurt pride I felt at this invasion of my privacy—after all, not one of the three of these people so dear to me had even seen my beau at home. Whose girl was I, anyway?

Now Pete Anderson waited. Pulling on my fur cap and mittens, I went out almost gaily—glad, glad to realize, at last, that I didn't have to tell anyone to wait while I grew up. Poor little Mother. Maybe she thought Pete's wealth would make me love him just like that![42] I didn't even feel angry with her anymore.

Hans led the other dogs off willingly, though under a strange driver. Wrapped warmly in the sleigh, I settled down a bit uneasily to enjoy the ride. The sun was beginning to show its long-absent face in lengthier stays each day, and it was always good to be out-of-doors if weather permitted.

Pointing out landmarks observed on previous rides or on hunting trips, I made an effort to be an agreeable companion to the older man. Back at the house, Pete had suggested taking a lunch, but my expressed preference for a hot lunch had apparently satisfied him. Rass had raised an eyebrow, for well he knew that a pocketful of raisins and a few nuts had been adequate lunch for many of my eight- or ten-mile walking trips.

At the end of an hour, Pete stopped the dogs beside a fallen log that lay just below the trail. He scraped the snow from the top of it, dusted it with his gloves, and sat down facing me. I chattered volubly about the returning birds, the glaciers we had passed, and the beautiful mountaintops—but it was of no use. Pete said rather nervously, "Peggy, I want to talk to you."

I looked at him thinking, "Oh, brother! This is it. I can't stop him, and I'll bet he has already said something to Mother—and she's for it!" A silly thought followed: "Mush on!"

Pete's face was serious and he said earnestly, "Peggy, I love you, and I want you to marry me." His face was crimson, but he went on, "I never knew such an unspoiled girl as you are, and I want you to be my wife."

I was ashamed of my first, frivolous thoughts, and now was thinking, "Please stop, Pete. I don't want to marry you. I don't love you. Please. Please." I started to say something, but he continued.

"I know I am older than you are, but does that matter so much after all? I would give you a home in Seattle, Minneapolis—my hometown—or anywhere else you wished. We could go Outside for the winter and live at the mine during the summer season." He took a quick breath and said urgently, "Could you answer me now, or do you want to think it over?"

Completely sobered by the man's earnestness and evident sincerity, I met his eyes and said quietly:

"I am sorry, Pete. It isn't altogether your age. I am too young to marry now. I want to finish school. Besides, when I do marry, I want to be very much in love, and I am not in love with you." My heart whispered, "But I am in love with someone else, I think."

I could see the muscles in Pete's jaws become rigid and he begged, "Couldn't you even think about it?"

I shook my head slowly. "Let's go back."[43]

Back in the house, no one could have guessed that our ride was anything more important to either of us than just an outing. We laughed and joked, and when after lunch Pete trudged off to Mastodon Creek, he was still wearing his snowpacks—the leather shoes forgotten in his knapsack.

After his solitary figure was out of sight, my imagination saw some small question marks curling around in the atmosphere of the cabin. Nothing was said, however, and I got very busy mending a woolen jacket.

When the supper dishes were out of the way and the big table was cleared, I sat down and wrote a letter. It was the first in many months to a certain young man in California.

Chapter 12

FINDING JIMMY MCCARTHY

O NE evening after supper, Uncle Ned looked up from the big ledger he was writing in and commented, "While the trail is still hard enough for the dogs, I think it would be well for me to take another load of material over to our assessment cabin. It will be there if there is any time to work it up before the mine opens here; if not, it can be used next winter."

Rass nodded, "Good idea."

Uncle Ned went on, "I think I'll come back by Jimmy McCarthy's place on the way home. He hasn't been here all winter, and I want to know how he is making out. It's only a few miles out of the way."

"How about me going along?" I asked eagerly. It was fine weather, cold but not windy, and I was always ready for a trip of any kind. Since most of my outings were made alone, to go with my favorite uncle would be a rare treat. I remembered Jimmy McCarthy's visit to us in the fall after we first arrived at Eagle. He was a tall, lanky, red-haired Irishman. His very red nose and many freckles had caused me to comment on them. Uncle Ned had laughed and said, "The nose color comes out of a bottle. Jimmy takes his whiskey straight and plenty of it."

Looking at me now, doubtfully, Uncle said, "You'd have to ride shanks pony [walk] all of the way over and part of the way back. It's a rather long trip—take all day."

"You wouldn't insinuate that I am unable to walk a mile or three," I jeered. I could see that he was pleased that I wanted to go, and I thought it wouldn't take much coaxing.

Mother urged, "Let her go, Ed, if she wants to. She's been walking that far every week, if not all in one day." She smiled at me when Uncle made no protest, "If you are going, young lady, you had better get to bed and no late reading tonight."

When we called the dogs to their harness the next morning, they came willingly, tails waving. They, too, seemed always eager for any excursion. Hans, the leader, rubbed against Uncle's leg, and after his harness was adjusted, sat down like a dignified old man to wait while Fox, Jeff, and Lion were readied. Curly old black Fritz smelled around anxiously until he got Uncle's attention. Looking at the eagerly wagging tail, he said kindly, "No, boy, you can't go today. It's too far for your poor old legs." The disconsolate old fellow, tail down like a sagging banner, went off to his kennel. I am sure that if there had been a door to its entrance, he would have slammed it behind him.

It was a pleasant trip with the dogs in fine fettle, though they soon learned that there was a full load to pull. Uncle Ned helped to boost the sled over unexpected rough spots and jumped on the step behind to break the speed on downgrades. The many rabbit tracks that crossed the trail were ignored by the dogs, and I wondered why they never offered to run off to follow them as they often did when Mother or I was driving. Did they guess that this was not a pleasure trip? Did they realize that it would be hard to drag a loaded sled off in pursuit of a leaping rabbit, or did they guess that Uncle would not stand for such foolishness?

Sometimes I led the procession, sometimes dropped behind, lifting the .22 rifle from the sled as it passed to practice. We were always shooting, either for game or targets. No one seemed to care how many .22 short or long cartridges were used. The idea was to be a good shot.

Uncle would say, "See that black spot on that rock? See if you can hit it." If my shot went wild, he would take the rifle and say patiently, "Let me show you how it's done," explaining, "if you get the bead right in the center of the sight and hold it there while you pull the trigger, you can't miss. Try again."

We rested frequently as the morning passed, and when finally we reached our destination, it was eleven o'clock.

Uncle Ned removed boards previously nailed across the door of the cabin, and I built a fire in the small iron stove to melt snow for coffee. While he unharnessed the dogs and stored the load in a lean-to built on the end of the cabin, there was time for the one-room cabin to warm up a bit.

I found a can of frozen pears on the shelf and decided to add them to our lunch. There was not a can-opener in sight so a sharp, short-handled miner's pick proved convenient to pierce a row of connecting holes around the lid. The fruit was delicious, if slightly mangled!

As soon as we had finished lunch and carefully scattered the hot embers from the fire in the snow outside, we reharnessed the team and started off across the country to the creek where Jimmy McCarthy lived. Free of the load, the dogs went faster, and it was nice to catch a short ride now and then. We had followed a frozen stream for several miles when Uncle stopped the dogs for a rest. We had had to drive up on the hillside to get around an impassable barrier of debris in the creek bed. He pointed off down a small ravine.

"Look down that draw—a bit to the right. Jimmy's cabin is just around that curve in the creek on the south bank."

As we got near enough to see the little log cabin clearly, Uncle Ned suddenly cried, "Whoa, boys." He peered intently at the small building and its surroundings and said, "Strange, no smoke coming out of the chimney. Snow all over the door, yard—looks like he isn't home. Maybe he went to Fairbanks," he said doubtfully, "but he doesn't have either a horse or a dog team. Mush, Hans," he ordered suddenly, and we made our way slowly down the incline. It was rocky and rather steep, and he braked the empty sled frequently so it would not advance on the wheel dog's heels.

We were a short way from the cabin, Uncle still looking concerned and puzzled, when he suddenly ordered sharply, "Whoa, Hans!" adding shortly, "You stay here, Peggy, with the dogs. I am going down to see what is going on down there."

The deserted-looking building stood on a flat ledge just above the creek. There was a wide, shallow place there where the stream (when flowing) changed its course slightly. There was snow everywhere, and a blanket of it entirely covered the roof of the small dwelling. The door was closed, but not boarded, as was often done when an owner was away for any length of time.

Uncle Ned covered the downward slope that separated us from Jimmy's cabin in long, stiff-legged leaps. When he reached the bottom, I was surprised to see him stop abruptly before reaching the building and peer intently at the snow-covered earth beside the creek. He looked up at me and shouted, "Stay there, Peggy. Don't come down." Then he went to the small cabin, opened the door, and disappeared inside.

A few minutes later he emerged, carrying a blanket. He went directly to the spot he had observed so intently before entering the cabin. As he prepared to spread the blanket carefully, I saw to my horror that what I had thought was a snow-covered log was a human form sprawled facedown almost in the frozen creek!

When Uncle rejoined me, he said grimly, "Well, Jimmy had one too many drinks this time. I found a whiskey bottle almost empty on the table along with a row of empties. Evidently, he ran outside in his long underwear and wool socks and fell down—probably too drunk to get up again. He is frozen stiff. No telling how long he has been there. Funny thing about his door being closed—guess he wanted to keep the cabin warm." Uncle shuddered. "Good Lord," he stammered, "a bird had picked one of his eyes out!"

"Mush, Hans," he started the team.

"Are you just going to leave him there?" I asked incredulously as we moved off.

"We'll send word to the marshal in Circle. Tomorrow is mail day. Rass and I will come back and bury him."[44]

Chapter 13

SPRING

THE daylight hours were gradually getting longer and brighter. Where not long before the snow had echoed "crunch, crunch" underfoot, now it hissed "slick, slick" in the middle of the day. More birds were flying north. Many stayed in our valley, but thousands more continued their purposeful flight.

One bright morning I went over to the barn as I often did to see to the horses. Their shelter, or dugout, was a small building of logs built largely under ground level. A ramp of roughly split saplings provided an entrance. The roof was thickly sodded, and the heavy door could be closed when the weather necessitated. With the heat from the horses' bodies and a thick layer of wild hay under their feet, they were comfortable during the coldest weather. Nature added protection from the arctic winter by a heavy coat of hair, which came out by handfuls as the weather warmed.

Nearing the corner of the stable on this spring morning, I saw a tuft of bright green leaves poking up through the snow. To a California Valley farm girl who had become a bit overwhelmed by the immensity of an all-white winter, that little cluster of live-looking vegetation seemed a treasure dropped right in my path.

Kneeling down, I was amazed to discover that it was indeed a growing plant, bravely lifting its head above the snow. Quickly I found a stick and dug the encircling snow away. The plant had a spindly little stem and could not stand alone, so I laid it carefully over in the snow, deciding then and there to dig the poor little stranger out of its cold bed and replant it in the house. Always-obliging Rass found a wooden packing crate and cut it down to fit one of the wide windowsills in the living-dining room where it was always warm.

By this time, Uncle Ned was poking a bit of fun at my weak-looking flower, but I brushed him aside. With a shovel it was possible to dig out some good soil from under the woodpile. After I warmed this good, loose loam in the oven, it was ready to go in the box over a layer of pebbles from my rock collection. Rass suggested some bits of charcoal, and these I was able to scratch out of the ash pile.

Carefully then, so as not to disturb the plant's root system, I got it out of the ground and into its new home. The fragile little stem needed support, so I fastened a string to the top of the windowsill and brought it down to a nail in the side of the box. I wound the spindly plant around the twine and fastened it securely with a bit of wool yarn.

After all of this preparation I waited expectantly for my plant to grow strong and sturdy. Instead, it went up and up its support! Side shoots appeared and dangled helplessly until they too were tied to more strands of twine and joined the others on the upward climb. By the end of the summer this strange vine completely filled the window with luxuriant foliage (but insignificant flowers). I had searched diligently, but unsuccessfully, for another specimen like this. We decided it must have grown from a seed from a bale of hay that came in originally from Canada. It was a conversation piece, and when anyone asked about it, my family always answered, "Why, that is Peggy's posy."

Chapter 14

CARIBOU HUNT

I N the midst of the preparation for the mine opening, the first caribou of the spring season were sighted on a hillside behind the diggings—just one pair.

Eagle Pass was the regular path for the semiannual migrations, and we had been watching daily for the seasonal run to begin. We had missed the main autumn trek by a few weeks. However, at that time by diligent hunts, the men had been able to get stragglers enough to provide fresh meat for the winter. By this time our supply had dwindled, and it would be wise to replenish, especially since there were extras to feed and the mining crew would be augmented later.

All through the winter, in fact since the day I had set foot on Alaska soil, the uncles (both crack shots themselves) had been teaching me the fine points of good shooting. They often set up targets to check on my progress and urged constant practice.

Now they seemed satisfied that I would be able to get the season's limit of caribou, which was three (either sex).

If I was skeptical, they jeered, "There'll be thousands—you couldn't possibly miss them all!"

So, now that the first animals had arrived, I was supposed to be given the chance to be the mighty hunter. Perhaps these two stragglers were scouts.

George Lorenz, who was working for Berry and Lamb, offered, "I will take you hunting, Peggy. I won't be needed here for an hour or two."

Armed with our rifles we set off, quickly working up the slope, maneuvering as quietly as possible to get near the caribou and still be upwind. We got occasional glimpses of the pair, but they were not aware of us, and they grazed quietly along as they moved slowly toward the hilltop.

At last George whispered, "There they are! Kneel down and get a good sight on the buck—he's the biggest."

I pulled down to a good bead and quickly pulled the trigger. Just as I fired, BANG!—another shot rang out simultaneously. Startled, I looked around to see smoke curling upward from the barrel of George's gun.

"I'm sorry, kid, I was afraid you'd miss him," he stammered.

We both looked at the buck, which had gone down immediately. We could see the doe leaping over the terrain, out of rifle shot already.

I was miffed, and said shortly, "How do you know *you* hit him?"

George said nothing, but started off up the hill, expecting me to follow. I didn't wish to argue with him about who killed the darn thing. Instead, I turned back down the hill, disappointed and disgruntled. Gun in hand, I went back home. I didn't like George too well anyway—he had been passing out a bit of "sweet talk" whenever the opportunity presented itself. Although he was tall, dark, and rather good-looking, he had a cast in one eye. My superstitious little grandmother had often warned, "Look out for a man with a cast in his eye."

When George got back to the house to get the horse to carry in the caribou, one of the men said, "Where's Peggy?"

Not knowing that I had come back unobserved and thinking I had reported what had happened, George said, "Oh, hell, I don't know who shot the damn thing!"

Then they guessed the truth and by supper time every man on the place had kidded George. "Such a mighty hunter! Sure a hero!" they said.

Some of the razzing I heard from my bedroom window with a great deal of satisfaction. It completely restored my good humor, and after a while I began to feel sorry. Poor George— he would hear about this the rest of the summer.

Our cranky neighbor, Mr. Bowman, who worked only enough to make eating possible and said that any man of sixty who had any sense would quit working, had been standing around enjoying George's discomfiture. The digs and jibes he was taking were highly amusing to the old man.

"Old Man Bo," as Uncle Ned called him, came back the next day and hunted me up. "I'll take you hunting, Peggy," he promised. "These young whipper-snappers are trigger-happy. We'll show 'em! Just you wait—there'll be a day soon. We'll show 'em."

In a few days a sizable herd of caribou showed up against the skyline on the ridge. Mr. Bo came puffing and panting up to our place. He had been almost running the two miles, knowing that if we had not sighted the animals in an hour or so, they would have moved out of sight.

We saddled up the horses and set out. It is a strange thing, but caribou are not afraid of horses, and if they do not get the human scent, one can ride fairly close to them. We rode for nearly an hour, getting nearer and in better position. As soon as we came within shooting range and could distinguish separate animals, we noticed that an unusually large buck seemed to be leading a herd of twenty or thirty caribou. He was a handsome fellow and carried a magnificent set of antlers.

When Mr. Bo figured we had gotten as near as we possibly could without disturbing our prey, we stopped the horses. I raised my safety and placed my finger firmly on the trigger. A tremor of excitement ran through me—I felt very confident—and wasn't he a beauty. I would shoot from the horse, as he had been trained for hunting. I got the sight dead center and quickly pulled the trigger. BANG! Almost like a duet, BANG! came an explosion just behind me.

I just looked at the old man numbly, then back to the huge caribou that had dropped in his tracks. The rest of the herd were leaping in all directions, their sharp hoofs crackling on the rocks.

Mr. Bo chuckled, "We got him, didn't we, gal?"

I said nothing. I was furious!

He said grandly, "If it's a little hole, you killed him. If it's a big hole, I got him." (I was shooting a .25-35 rifle, he a big .45.)

"Agreed," I said quickly, for I didn't see how I could have missed. Both of us dismounted and tied our horses loosely to some brush, then we hurried to the fallen caribou. There was a nice, clean little hole where the animal's jugular vein had been cut and his blood was spilling out redly on the ground. Mr. Bo turned him over—no other mark was to be found.

I looked at Mr. Bo, triumph in my eyes. He straightened up, dusted off his pants, and said cockily, "Well, I guess I killed him. My rifle would have made a little hole carrying this far. Ain't he a beaut?"

I couldn't decide whether I felt worse because I was cheated out of my big triumph or because the beautiful animal was dead.

Together we got the heavy carcass on Old Man Bo's horse, and leading him, we went off down the hillside.

Mr. Bo bragged to the men about the caribou. It really was a fine specimen. He left most of the meat with us, for with summer coming, one man would need little without refrigeration.

It was only after a little prodding that Uncle Ned heard the particulars of my second big game hunt. He was indignant. "Why, that old so-and-so! He can't shoot for sour beans. No wonder he left so much meat. Well, I'll take you out next time myself."

There came a day soon when he kept his word. I got the season's limit and found it was not much fun after all. When Uncle sensed my revulsion at all of the gore, he said gently, "Well, you know, we have to eat."

I nodded numbly.

Chapter 15

GEORGE

GEORGE LORENZ began following me around, first with his eyes, then with his big, clumsy feet. He was always asking me to go hiking with him, either on Sunday or after working hours, but I managed to avoid him. Like the little pig in the nursery tale, I went earlier.

Mother couldn't understand my attitude and chided, "Why, Peggy, George is a nice young man."

"Young?" I objected, "He's thirty-two! He told me so last week. That's almost twice my age. I just don't want him to get any ideas. No more proposals, please, they embarrass me." I went on, "He's much too old, even if I liked him—which I don't. He seemed like fun at first, but now he is too serious." Striking a pose, I said dramatically, "Remember what Grandma says— quote 'Be cautious in dealing with a man who has a cast in his eye!' George has a cast in his eye, so there!"

Mother laughed merrily, "Such nonsense." Our laughter mingled and the subject was dropped.

One fine afternoon when a long hike was appealing, I climbed up the hillside behind the cabins and sat down on a rock to dangle my feet over its edge and to enjoy the peaceful scene below. The white tents of the mine workers and the silvery stream of the water from the hydraulic nozzle were part of the picture. I was thoroughly enjoying the solitude when I saw George laboring up toward my rock. I was disconcerted and disgusted. He was supposed to be working! "Just because he is the straw boss," I thought angrily.

"Hello," George greeted cheerfully as he came near. "Enjoying yourself?"

"I was," I said to myself. Aloud I commented, "There is a very nice view of the mines from here."

"I didn't come up here to enjoy the view," he laughed, "and you know it. Why have you been avoiding me?" he demanded. Without waiting for an answer he declared indignantly, "I won't bite you."

"Look," I said shortly, "I'm not afraid you will bite me. I just like to hike alone."

"Come on now," he grinned placatingly, "listen to me and pay attention. I have something on my mind." He hesitated, then blurted, "I'm in love with you."

"But George, I am not in love with you. Let's just forget it."

"Wait a minute—don't get mad," he begged. "I am deadly serious. I want you to marry me."

"Marry you? I am too young to marry you or anyone else. Please don't talk about it."

"I will too talk about it," he went on doggedly. "My mother was only sixteen when she married Dad and she got along all right—had six sons—all of them over six feet tall now."

"Where are your other brothers?" I asked, trying to steer him away from the subject of marriage.

"Most of them live in California. Our home is in Red Bluff."

"What are their names and are you the tallest?" I went on quickly.

"You should see the space we cover lying on the ground in a line," he began. "Just a minute," he ordered. "Don't try to change the subject!" Soberly then, he said, "By the time the mine closes this fall and I go Outside, you'll change your mind. We could get married in Circle," he continued wistfully, "and go Out together."

"I am sure I won't change my mind," I said definitely. "Now I have to go home and help with supper." I slid quickly off the rock and challenged, "I'll race you to the house." And with that I ran off down the slope.

"You're early, Honey," Mother remarked as she looked up from her needlework. She looked like a little queen. Her curled pompadour was in shining order, and the frilly white blouse she wore was as fresh as morning cream. The long, dark skirt covered her ankles sedately, and her prettily shod feet rested primly on a fat hassock. To see this small, slender woman in her feminine daintiness, I found it hard to realize her wiry endurance or to visualize her an hour later as she would be in an all-enveloping apron, preparing a huge meal for ten hungry miners.

I sighed. Remembering the pretty dresses she had made so lovingly for me just hanging in my closet brought the fleeting thought that it was just possible that Mother might be a bit disappointed in her "outdoor girl." Heck! Who wanted to be dressed up all afternoon—not me. House dresses in the morning, hiking clothes for afternoon. It was enough to dress up a bit at supper time or for the evening.

I went to my room and freshened up quickly, and when my clothes were changed, went to sit near Mother.

"Mother," I began hesitantly, "I wish George would let me alone. Can't you do something?"

Mother dropped her sewing into her workbasket and looked at me seriously for a long minute. Smiling then, she got up and went to the cupboard under the bookcase and got out her zither. In her chair again with the flat instrument on her lap, she pushed the black bone pick on her finger and gently played a few chords. The sweet melody hummed around the room while she sang softly, smiling mischievously:

"In the spring a young man's fancy . . . "

"Oh, Mother," I laughed protestingly. "Spring is long gone, summer is here, and George is an old goose. He asked me to marry him today! Imagine! And he is thirty-two!"

Mother's eyes twinkled mischievously as she said, "You can't blame him for trying, dear."

I mimicked George's manner to tell her. "My mother was only sixteen and she was not too young to have six tall sons." Then added, "Phooey! Who wants to get married at sixteen, anyway? My mother was twenty-two and look what happened to her—five babies and she was dead at thirty-five! I don't think I'll ever get married. I sure don't want any children of mine to have a stepmother like my own."

Mother sobered immediately. "You must remember, dear, that although by our standards you are too young for marriage, many of the men who live here were borne by mothers younger than you are. Many of their parents came from other lands, too. We neither arrange marriages nor barter girls in America as many in other races do. Our own girls," she continued, "are free to choose or reject." She then said earnestly, "As long as you keep yourself to yourself, you have that privileged freedom, too. A man pays you his highest compliment when he asks you to marry him. Never scoff, but be grateful that you are desirable. Wouldn't it be terrible," she teased with a smile, "if you turned out to be an old maid? As for George," she comforted, "he will leave as soon as the mine closes."

Chapter 16

HELEN'S VISIT—MY BIRTHDAY

HELEN CALLAHAN came to visit. Sensing that I was getting terribly lonely for the company of young people, Mother had sent for this young, part-Indian girl who was very dear to her to help me celebrate my birthday.

She was the charming young woman I'd enjoyed meeting in Circle. Her stepfather, Dan Callahan, was dead[45] and Helen and her mother had a very fine business in Fairbanks making beautiful garments of fur. Helen's skin was a shade darker than olive, her hair was black, and her eyes were dark and deep. She had a merry, infectious laugh that revealed fascinating dimples.

Helen shared my household duties willingly, and every day we hurried through them and dashed outside. Several days I led her to the top of the second ridge above the creek where, on a very clear day, beautiful Mt. McKinley had once revealed its towering, white peaks—but she laughed at my recurring disappointment. The day was never just right for me to show her this wondrous sight. At last she explained her amusement at my discomfiture. "I have seen it many times. This is my country. Remember?"

One day we discovered a pair of fine snowshoes in the storage cabin. There were others there in need of repair. Luckily, Hooch Albert came to see us that day and was delighted to unearth some leather thongs from his pack and repair them.

Hooch was a familiar figure and one of the most fascinating callers we had. He was French-Canadian and a skilled taxidermist. The government would not allow him to pursue his favorite occupation of whiskey-making, however. "By Gar, your Uncle Sammie, she is very hard on me," he laughed.[46]

Helen taught me how to snowshoe with some speed by using side lurching steps. I fell on my stomach or back, got awkwardly on my feet again, and we laughed until we were weak.

Later I showed Helen the glacier down the creek. "I have an idea!" she said, exulted. "Get two gold pans and some pieces of old blanket. Small pillows will do if you can't find any old woolen scraps."

Our little glacier filled a small canyon and spilled out into a flat, lake-like expanse. In summer the creek flowed along one edge of the icy mass. No one knew how long it had been there, but until that year, 1910, it had never thawed. Much of the glacier was shaded by a steep, high hill. The ice on the flat expanse was ideal for skating, but we did not intend to skate that day.

Large air bubbles came up under the ice here and there (maybe forty or fifty feet apart), forcing it into dome-like knobs until each finally broke under pressure. A ridgy seam remained on one side and this, when refrozen, was rough enough to provide a footing by which to reach the top. Carrying our gold pans, we selected the largest dome and struggled to the top. Arriving there we folded the woolen blanket sections and laid them in the pans. Very carefully then we sat down in the gold pans and lifted our feet above the slick ice. A little push with our mittened hands on the ice on either side of our bodies— and away we went down the glassy surface. The short incline provided momentum enough that we were carried far out on the frozen lake.

On other bright days we took our rifles and went hunting. It had been most interesting to see the ptarmigan change their brown summer feathers to a snow-white coat in winter. It was hard to see them against the snow if they were quiet. Often though, one could hear a covey of them chattering (when not in alarm) like a group of happy children.

Since our family didn't relish the flesh of the abundant snowshoe rabbit, ptarmigan was a welcome change from caribou or moose, our principal fresh meat.

Helen knew so very much about the little animal creatures, especially the ones that we never saw, that she was able to tell their exciting adventures by little tracks along the way. She knew all of the birds, all about the seasons, and many other mysteries of the wilderness.

She never spoke of her people and, though there were endless questions I would like to have asked, I never did. Once in a moment of confidence when we were discussing our futures, Helen declared, "I will never marry." At my startled, "Why?" she answered sadly, "I would never bring a child into the world who felt as lost as I do. I will not live with the Indians, and some of the white people do not accept me."

I was stunned! I had never lived among people not of my own race and had thoughtlessly never even considered such a calamity as this.

One evening during Helen's visit, there came a knock at our door. There stood a big, stout, red-faced Englishman who came to see her. She was quite embarrassed, but we all came to her rescue. We could see that she was not very happy about his presence and would not allow herself to be left alone with him. I poked a little fun at her after the man finally left, and she explained, "He proposes to me every spring—four years now." She laughed and said, "Could you imagine me marrying him? He is deathly afraid of a mouse!"

On my birthday, Mother gave me a fat gold nugget that Pete Anderson had left for that day. Helen shut herself up in my room and carefully lined a lovely birch bark basket with blue China silk. I still treasure this sweet basket. Mother made a yummy, big cake with candles and fixin's. Uncle Ned said sadly, "My little pal is growing up." As for me, I thought jubilantly, "One more year and I will be my own boss!"

Helen and I spent three delightful weeks together, but one bright morning she and Uncle Alf rode off on the horses to Circle where Helen's sister lived.

Chapter 17

AMERICAN NATIVE

As I sat by the window one busy morning picking over some dried beans, I caught a glimpse of a strange man, going around the cabin to the kitchen door. There was a quiet conversation between Mother and the caller. Soon I heard her promise, "All right, Clark, this afternoon after my work is done. About two o'clock will be all right."

The man answered gratefully, "Thank you, Mrs. Garner. Thank you very much."

"Tsk, tsk, who were you making dates with?" I teased after the man had gone. Mother shook some flour on the dough board and went on with her interrupted pie-making while she explained.

"Oh, that was Clark, a trapper who lives over in the next valley across the mountain. He wants me to take some pictures of his four-year-old daughter to send to his mother. He married a native Indian girl a few years ago and has never been home since."

"Where is home?" I asked curiously.

Mother's reply surprised me. "England. Evidently he comes from a prominent and wealthy family there, for the picture he once showed me of his boyhood home was one of a huge mansion set in beautifully landscaped, spacious grounds. It really looked like a castle. He said, somewhat bitterly, when he showed me the picture that he was a younger son. Since the elder son in an English family inherits, the younger ones are supported by a small allowance or commission and are often called 'commission men.' It is more comfortable for the lucky one if the younger brothers are far away. There are many of these men in British colonies and territories and a few around here. Do you remember Mr. Elliott, who called on Helen when she was here? He is one of them too."

"What an unfair deal!" I said indignantly.

Mother continued, "Clark has always spoken so lovingly of his mother the few times that I have seen him. Now he wants to see her so badly because she is getting very old. Evidently he disgraced his family in some way, for he told me they had disinherited him entirely many years ago. Perhaps he thinks if his family knew that he had married and had a child, they would forgive whatever offense he had committed and ask him to come home, if only for a visit."

"What kind of a man is this Clark, anyway?" I asked curiously.

"He is said to have done very well trapping. His wife must have taught him that. How else would an educated Englishman know how to make a living in that manner? The worst things that we know about Clark are that he is very dirty about his clothing and person, and that he is not very kind to his wife. In fact, he beat her up about a year ago. Poor little thing," Mother said sympathetically. "She was only about fourteen or fifteen years old when he married her and she has always had to work so very hard. She does all of the cleaning and dressing after Clark brings the animals in from his traplines. She also tans the hides from the larger animals like beaver and moose and from these she makes gloves, moccasins, and other garments. When Ed heard about the episode of the beating, he and a neighbor went there and told him that if it ever happened again, they would blister his bareness until he couldn't sit down. They check on him frequently, too," she smiled, "and he does seem to be a little more considerate of her."

"Do you think he would take his wife and child to England if he did go?" I asked.

"Oh, no," she said decidedly. "He would think up some reason for leaving them at home."

I washed the beans and put them on the stove to cook. "Now I suppose I have heard what the life of the wife of a Squaw Man (as they call them) is like. If you ask me, a Native girl is a fool to marry a white man. If she married a man of her own race, at least he would not be ashamed of her, even if she did have to do all of the work."

"Wait a minute, Honey," Mother reminded me. "You have never lived where two races lived side by side. All white men are not like Clark, by any means. Many of them have married Native girls and lived happy, meaningful lives, proud of them and of their families. They have provided clean, comfortable homes and seen to it that their children got the best possible education that was available. Some of them send to the outside world for books with which to teach not only the three Rs but something about the ways and culture of their own native homelands. Remember, we are all of the same physical makeup under the outer layer of flesh. The main differences among peoples and races are those of education, environment, and of course, climate. Many of the children of interracial marriages become brilliant students and fine citizens. The very fact that their not-too-distant ancestors lived close to nature gives them a broader and deeper insight into the meaning of life. Lecture ended; class dismissed," Mother said suddenly, laughing a bit at her own earnestness. She left with me many new things to puzzle about.

After I returned from my hike that afternoon, I quizzed Mother about her photographic appointment.

"I was disgusted," she admitted. "Clark had put so much flour on the poor little tot's face that she looked like a small, frightened mummy. Her clothes were suitable for his probable purpose, though. She had a little new mail-order coat on with a pretty bonnet that almost hid her pasty, white face. I couldn't help but imagine how cute she would look with her own little skin coat, beaded boots, and mittens."

"And a parka hood with fur around her face," I said. "Mother, do you think he is very mean to her?"

"No, I am sure he isn't. She was frightened and shy, but he was very patient when she cried a little, and she clung to him for comfort and reassurance."

"Of course, the mother wasn't in the picture," I surmised.

"Oh, no. She didn't even come. If Clark had been wise, he would have brought her along. We would have been able to get a more natural picture."

Chapter 18

Hint of Homesickness

THE mine was in full swing and the sun almost forgot to leave the land. It came down to the horizon, disappeared for a few hours, then reappeared almost in the same spot, to repeat a slightly longer cycle the following day.

The weather was warm, and it was wonderful to discard extra layers of clothing. Soft cotton next to my flesh felt like silk after the scratchy, woolen winter undergarments.

Great soaking rains blew up suddenly and as quickly disappeared. The longer hours of welcome sunshine speedily dried up the muddy terrain.

Our increased cooking chore, brought on by a completed crew of six mine workers (making us ten in all), was now routine and well organized. Each day, as soon as the midday duties were finished, I was out and away on my solitary excursions. If my mood turned to the hills, I wore leather boots, but rubber ones were better for the days when I roamed along the streamlets, exploring, or wandered through the swampy places.

Now that the snow was gone, except in the shadiest places, wildflowers were popping up everywhere. There were Iceland poppies that bowed gracefully before the clean wind. The colorful fireweed flung down boundless red patches of brilliance in the sun. Tiny little forget-me-nots of daintiest blue nodded shyly from low-mounded clumps. Wild honeysuckle clung to any tall support and smiled down at the swaying penstemon and saucy

Johnny-jump-ups. There were countless thousands of white and yellow daisies and blue arcrotis. Many brilliant lovelies, complete strangers to me, highlighted the colorful patterns on the hills and valleys.

The perfumed wind ruffled my hair mischievously and often blew my hat off and rolled it down the hillside. I let it lie while I sat on a rocky prominence and experienced pure ecstasy. Breathing in the awesome majesty and beauty of this strange land, I was lost in daydreaming.

Thinking over tales heard of extreme hardships of dauntless pioneer stampeders, I settled one point to my own satisfaction. All of this grandeur of mountaintops, verdant valleys where wild hay grew luxuriantly, the flowers, the abundance of life-sustaining wild game—these and all of the other tangibles and intangibles were the just rewards, the final fulfillment of dreams—dreams that lured men, and women, too, from factory or farm, from schoolrooms or merchant ships, to follow the beckoning hand of adventure. What hardship and pain, what heartbreak and disillusion was the dream's end for so many.

There were some who longed only for gold, but there were those others who scarcely realized that the land with its endless fascinations was the siren who held them here, failing to hold them for a time, perhaps, but luring them back, in spirit if not in reality, to the place where, of all their life's experiences, they most felt a nearness to their Maker. Here, surely, was God's domain, and one proffered reverent thanks for a glimpse of a quiet paradise.

The bases of the nearest hills, standing in colorful masses of wildflowers, gave access to the lower mountains. The latter seemed to stand guard over the entrance and to allow only those of real courage and fortitude to reach the top of the mighty range beyond. Their snowy, jagged peaks were etched in serrated patterns against a turquoise sky. Often, fat puffs of cloud swirled around them, allowing only tantalizing glimpses of the highest pinnacles. Too often a pale, gray-blue bank obliterated the entire higher range.

Sitting silently, I gazed out over the little valley at whose feet the busy stream ran. Eagle Creek—how apt a name when it had run free and unfettered in the long ago. Now it was narrowly confined into a foaming silver tongue that licked voraciously into the vein of gold. It washed the natural verdure to a mass of mud, gravel, rocks, and debris into the streambed.

Thoughts turned to my home and brothers in California— would Ruby make the track team? Why had Alva quit school? Was it because Father needed him on the ranch, or were trig and German just too much for his happy soul? How was Father, anyway? There was never any direct message; only from the boys' letters did I learn that he was well and working hard as usual. How was Claude getting along in the big city of San Francisco? He had gone there to work some time before.

My heart protested, but I thought, too, of Lily my stepmother—too bad she hated me so. I wished fervently that this was not so. In my early teens once I had ventured to put my arms around her, asking, "Don't you think we could get along better?"

Spitefully the answer came, "Well, I guess we could, if you'd behave yourself."

Frustrated, unhappy at her rebuff and longing for harmony, I had thought hopelessly, "What have I done? What can I do?"

"Enough of this!" I scolded my straying thoughts. "That is all so far away." Forthwith, I swallowed the small lump in my throat and stood—a lap-full of flower petals falling in a shower at my feet.

Retrieving my hat, I started for home, stopping only to gather an armload of wildflowers. Mother loved flowers too, and I kept fresh ones in the house as long as there were any to be found. If, on one of these thoughtful days, I presented them to her with a fervent kiss, she seemed to understand that I appreciated her kindness and love.

Chapter 19

MIGRATION

IT was as exciting to see the midnight sun in June of 1910 as when I first saw it in Circle the previous summer. My personal pattern of activities continued about as usual. George and I had declared a sort of truce. He could join the family for an evening of cards or dancing—a friend, that was all.

As the mining crew grew in numbers, there was more cooking to do, but Rass, bless him, managed to help with our breadbaking after his day's work. Mother's good management ensured free afternoons for her and for me, and I never tired of riding horseback or hiking over the hills that bordered Eagle Creek. One day on the very crest of one of them, what seemed a miracle appeared. In a shallow depression, a wide, compact patch of forget-me-nots lifted their pretty blue faces to the Alaska sky. There were no others nearby, although I had found a few in another valley, and I wondered if a bird had once dropped a tiny seed here and that over countless seasons the little plants had multiplied to form this large azure pillow.

Mr. Clarence Berry came in July to check on the mining activities. After the time Uncle Ned and Rass spent building the snug log cabin for the Berrys' comfort, we were all disappointed that they stayed only two days and then went on to the Berry and Lamb properties near Miller House. We thought perhaps the fact that their furniture, when unpacked, was found to be cut, slashed, and otherwise marred by labor strikers when in transit might have had something to do with their short stay.[47]

Over the season Uncle Alf carried the "cleanups"[48] in leather pouches to Fairbanks, and all seemed pleased with the "takes." We had a bit of excitement when a strange man who looked like a thug suddenly appeared one morning about three o'clock at the mine as Uncle Ned played the stream from a hydraulic nozzle over a fresh cut. The clatter of the shifting, dislodged rocks and gravel prevented announcement of his coming. Naturally, Uncle was surprised when the man stepped close to his side with no word of greeting and stood with his hands in his pockets, closely observing the operation. We had heard of some gold thefts around the country, and Uncle's first thought was of the recent cleanup and of its safety in Fairbanks. However, in his usual, friendly way, he shouted, "Hello, there." There was no response either by word or gesture for a long ten or fifteen minute interval. Abruptly then, the stranger turned and made his way up the short incline to the trail and out of sight. If the man came near the cabins, no one knew of it, and we could only guess at his strange behavior.

I had been wondering about the blueberries as I found a few scrawny plants in our valley. One sunny day, Uncle Ned, Rass, and I rode horseback over to a spot across the ridge where Rass had got our winter supply the previous summer. The luscious berries, fully ripened and big as peas, were so thick in places we were able to put our containers under the laden branches and knock them off with sticks. Our full pails were a bit unwieldy on the ride home, but Mother greeted us with a promise of fresh shortcake for supper.

Hiking one late August afternoon, I suddenly became aware that it was barely possible to find a few fresh flowers for our table. The wind rattled seedpods on tall, gaunt stems as if to warn quietly that summer was almost over. The ptarmigan were showing a few white feathers among the brown and gray ones, for soon they would be as white as the winter snow.

When the mailman came, the letters from my high school friends were full of their parties and plans for school opening in September, and about that time several of the mine workers began talking about going Outside and of their plans for the winter. Winter?

As suddenly as I had made my decision to come to Alaska, I realized that I, too, wanted to go Outside to see my family and friends, to resume the six-mile daily buggy rides to high school and probably take some moonlight ones with Earl.

But how could I tell these dear ones who had been so kind and loving that now I wanted to leave this wonderful, free life and return home—home to an uncertain welcome from my step-mother but to the assured and constant regard of my father and brothers, to youthful companionship, and to school? Somewhat to my surprise that word "school" loomed large among the wishes that confused and enticed. Somehow, a guilty feeling of possible disloyalty and unappreciation prevented a spoken word of my mental torment and fears that it soon would be too late.

Inexorably, September came and at last, one day when Uncle Ned asked solicitously, "Why are you so quiet, Peggy? Don't you feel well?" I blurted out, "Uncle Neddie, I want to go home!"

He had just come into the cabin, and both he and Mother looked at me in astonishment. Was I joking? After what seemed to me a very long time, he said quietly, "What do you want to go home for, Peggy?"

"I want to go back to school," was the honest answer.

"You are sure?" he questioned.

"Yes, I am sure."

He looked then at Mother, whose eyes were full of tears, but he promised, "All right, we can send you home in Mr. and Mrs. Lamb's care, and if you ever want to come back, just let us know."

It was only a few days later until all arrangements for my trip Outside had been made. Foolishly, I destroyed the precious collection of wildflowers that I had pressed and dried during the summer. What had seemed a most interesting hobby now appeared unimportant and childish.

As Uncle Ned and I rode away on horseback, my blurred last look was of Timmy, my now half-grown malamute, sitting soberly on his haunches, watching anxiously. My little Alaskan mother was nowhere in sight.

PHOTOGRAPHS

Peggy Rouch, dressed for a school play in Fresno, California.

Peggy's uncle, Alf Garner. This picture is thought to have been taken in Dawson or Nome, about 1900.

The wedding picture of Nellie and Ed Garner, taken in Hanford, California, sometime before 1897.

The Garner party on the steamer *Cottage City* in 1909. *On the boom behind the mast:* Andy and Jim Woods. *In front, left to right:* Bill Cressman, Captain Joel P. Geer, Nellie Garner, Peggy Rouch, Ed Garner, Rass Rassmussen, and Alf Garner.

At the Skagway Hotel – *in the front, left to right:* Peggy Rouch, Nellie Garner, and Olive Geer. *In the back, left to right:* Ed Garner, M. Clark, Captain Joel P. Geer, Andy Woods, Rass Rassmussen, and Sam Warren.

Peggy indulges in target practice at Miles Canyon while waiting for spring breakup.

The Garner party tries out the boats they built at Whitehorse on the Yukon River.

The Garner party hits the ice of Lake Laberge (five miles wide and thirty miles long) and finds it slow going with no wind for their sails.

Finally they stop for a welcome lunch break. Shortly thereafter they were rescued by Indian freighters with dog teams.

With the help of the Indian freighters and their dogs, the Garner party get their supplies across Lake Laberge.

The Circle waterfront in 1913, with Al and the Northern Commercial manager standing in front. It looked about the same when the Garner party arrived in 1909, a sleepy contrast to its heyday just before the turn of the century when the population was about 1,000.

Peggy, *left,* and her good friend Helen Callahan, who was born and raised in the area.

Peggy struggles over Eagle Summit en route to the Berry camp at Eagle Creek, carefully balancing her family's fragile "Morning Glory Bell" Victrola horn. The date was September 17, 1909.

Later the Garners photographed the treasure installed in their new living room, ready for some gala musical entertainment.

Alf Garner with his trusty dog team at Eagle Creek.

Alf and Rass Rassmussen at a rude camp on Birch Creek. They prospected there in the fall of 1909. Dead ptarmigan decorate their chopping block, in preparation for the next meal.

Peggy and her new malamute puppy, Timmy, during the 1909 Christmas celebration.

Nellie Garner enjoys rare leisure at the gold camp, fashionably dressed, as always. She also played the zither to amuse herself and her family.

Musical entertainment was much appreciated in the isolated gold camp. Here a Mr. Green plays the trombone, accompanied by "Hooch" Albert on the banjo.

Men readily shared the housework in winter's off season. Rass Rassmussen and the Garner men tackle the ironing in the living room of the Berry camp.

This photo captures the homemade fun the Berry camp residents manufactured during the long, hard winters. *From left:* Nellie Garner with family friend Rass Rassmus̀sen, *center,* and Nellie's husband, Ed, *right,* backed by "Hooch" Albert (hands near Ed's shoulders).

The Eagle Creek social set emerges from a wintry brunch for a photograph outside the home of Mr. and Mrs. Ed Garner one snowy morning during the winter of 1909–10. Ed is at the far left. Nellie wears the white apron and Alf peers up from the back. Peggy, who is missing, either had kitchen duty or was drafted as photographer. Note the ratio of men to women is nineteen to three.

"Hooch" Albert Fortier was a favorite of the Garners and also a well-known pioneer. He had come into the Fortymile area about 1894 and was well known and liked in all the gold camps from Circle to Dawson. Shown here leaving the Berry camp, he appears to be traveling light, but one would suspect some of his renowned home brew is on the sled.

Despite the fact they lived just a few miles south of the Arctic Circle, Ed and Nellie Garner and Peggy usually traveled to social events in style.

Charles Lamb, Clarence Berry's partner, built the first elegant board house in the area near Miller Creek for his wife. Celebrating the housewarming are, *left,* Mrs. Mildred Kelly, *center*, Mrs. Lamb, and, *far right,* Ed Garner.

Clarence Berry, already wealthy from Klondike gold discoveries and a petroleum company, did not spend much time on his Alaska claims. This photo was taken with his wife during a brief visit to Eagle Creek in 1910.

Here Nellie takes a rare turn at hydraulicking, the technique by which gold was extracted at the Berry camp. Tailings were moved by water through a long sluice box, which pressured the gold to drop to the bottom.

Alf Garner, one of the best shots in the territory, was elected to take the results of the Garners' first cleanup for Berry to the bank. According to a note in the family album, he was carrying $20,000 in gold.

After mining operations wound down, the Garners liked to vacation at Circle Hot Springs, then a rustic homestead.

Despite the primitive setting, Nellie and Peggy dressed in the latest fashion to entertain the usual raft of friends, seen dimly through the steam. Eventually the Garners hoped to buy the hot spring homestead and operate it as a roadhouse.

The Berry camp, photographed from a steep hill behind it in August of 1995, looks almost exactly as it did when Peggy left it in 1910. At close range, however, it is obvious that most of the buildings are weathered beyond repair.

Author Peggy Rouch Dodson looks thoughtful on the event of her 102nd birthday in 1995. Still lively in mind and spirit, she worked on the final editing of this book.

APPENDIX A
WHAT HAPPENED AFTERWARD

THE otherwise enviable marriage of Ed and Nellie Garner was never to be blessed by children. Peggy Rouch was as close to a daughter as Nellie Garner would ever have, and Nellie knew it. The girl's sudden decision to leave Alaska must have been doubly wrenching because it also deprived her foster mother of female company so valued in country populated almost solely by men.[49] Goodbyes were too much for Nell when the time came. Proud and perhaps unsure of controlling her emotions, she did not see her niece off, but she never argued with Peggy's logic in leaving.

Earlier that year, one of the Garners' many visitors at Eagle Creek, a well-educated "remittance man" from England, had taken interest in Peggy, and when he learned she was not Nellie's true daughter, he had a serious talk with the girl.

"What are you doing here?" he asked. "Why aren't you in school?"

It was a question that had been bothering Peggy too, and the Englishman's earnest concern set her thinking.

"You know it's a sin to waste a brain," he told her.

Since Peggy had no chance of completing her education in the Circle district, which had no high school, returning to her family in California seemed the best solution. And it must have been obvious to Nellie after her niece had turned down the most eligible bachelors in the region that, despite all Nellie's attempts at matchmaking, Peggy had her heart set on Earl Dodson, her letter-writing beau back home.

However, Peggy remained unusually close to her foster family, given the distance between California and Alaska. The Garners usually visited her on their occasional trips Outside, and otherwise they kept in touch via the erratic mail service.

Life in the mining region continued to be exciting. Alf wrote Peggy in August of 1911 that they'd had the driest summer on record, making hydraulic mining difficult. But he also reported with satisfaction that their first cleanup had netted about $18,000. Hooch Albert was going to San Francisco for a few days, he added, saying he'd believe it when he saw it.[50]

Alf, who was one of the deadliest shots in the district, had been earning his living as a game warden but quit that summer to go back to mining when the government cut his wage to $175 a month. Later he would invest with Archie Muir in Garner & Muir, a saloon in Circle City.

Alf Garner was also deputized as a guard by Marshal A. H. Hansen to help escort seven prisoners to the federal jail near Fairbanks. "Two of the prisoners were insane: Joseph Van Kowski and A. E. McMullen," the *Fairbanks Daily Times* noted.

> Van Kowski was brought from a place between Mouse Point and Kokrines and seems to be unbalanced on the subject of religion.

> He believes that he is a prophet and a seer and that he can not only foretell the future events, but can look beneath the moss and see the yellow gold effectively hidden from other mortals.

> In this connection it is interesting to note that Van Kowski is reputed to have found pay on a creek below Mouse Point, in a locality that has always been passed up by prospectors as unworthy of investigation. Down the river where the circumstances are well known, it is

said the pay is there to show for itself and that Kowski is an old prospector and has been industrious and energetic.

Young McMullen was formerly jail guard at Iditarod and it is said that guarding of the insane there served to unbalance him. His brother started out with him but he became so bad that they had to turn him over to federal authorities at [Ft.] Gibbon. He has given some trouble on the recent trip. . . ."[51]

When Marshall A. H. Hansen later wrote about his Alaska experiences, he devoted considerable space to Alf's prowess as a lawman and their adventures in taking in other difficult prisoners, undoubtedly in the off-mining season.[52]

Meanwhile, Ed and Nellie Garner leased Circle Hot Springs and took over winter management. Nellie's enthusiastic letters detail the lively social whirl. In 1911 there were the usual holiday parties, and a miner who returned from a visit Outside with the Berrys and the Lambs taught them the latest dances—the tango and the "Hesitation Waltz." "The Deadwood crowd of about twenty were here ten days. Well, that is all we did. I like the new dances much better than I do the old ones," Nell confessed. "We hardly took time to eat or sleep while they were all here."

In March of 1914, the Mammoth Creek Mining Company sold all its claims on Mammoth and Porcupine Creeks to C. J. Berry. The president of the Mammoth Creek enterprise was listed as William C. Leak and its secretary as Charles Lamb. Thus ended Lamb's substantial venture in the area, and the lovely house he built his wife at Miller Creek became known as the Berry House.

That summer, Nellie confided to Peggy she and Ed planned to make an offer on the hot springs that fall, although Ed would continue to work for Berry. She was also hopeful at this time that Alf, a lifelong bachelor who had originally come north because of a broken heart, might have found a potential wife. "He thinks an awful lot of a little girl just nineteen years old. A Miss Smith, she is so cute. She just thinks Uncle Al is the only one." Nothing came of either venture.

Later that year, sickness—perhaps the influenza epidemic—swept the area. There were two deaths in five days, including Mr. Bayless, leaving his wife devastated. Postmistress Dodson died seeking medical treatment outside the territory.

Helen Callahan moved to Fairbanks, and Nellie speculated (correctly) that she wouldn't be back to Circle. "Nelse (her teamster brother-in-law) and her, I guess haven't got along very well." Then, shortly after the death of his first wife, Mildred Kelly, who with her husband had run the tavern at Miller House, Jay Kelly remarried.

"Mr. Kelly is a papa. They have a nice little girl born in Fairbanks," Nellie wrote Peggy. "I wonder now if our dear little Mrs. Kelly was living, what she would think? This one is so young and has everything and never a thing to do. While the other one worked so hard and saved for this one to spend the money."[53]

As usual, Nellie signed her letter, "Lovingly, Mother," but there is a subtle new woman-to-woman tone in her correspondence, for by 1914 "little Peggy" had definitely grown up.

En route south in the late fall of 1910, armed with nine boxes of chocolates received as farewell gifts, escorted by Charles Lamb and his wife, Peggy was upset to find herself billeted in the bridal suite on the ship out of Skagway with Mary, the prostitute she had first seen at Harrington's mine. The best the captain could do, apparently because of crowded conditions, was tell the woman that she would not be able to do business on this trip. And things did not improve when Peggy got home to her family ranch at Kingsburg, California.

Her stepmother, blatantly antagonistic as usual, made off with her gold nugget bracelet the night of her arrival, and at the same time Peggy learned her father had sold her beloved pony. Shortly thereafter, the family asked her to care for her dying grandfather in Fresno, and she gave up classes to comply.

Finally, in the fall of 1911, she was allowed to attend a new high school in Kingsburg, and it was everything she had hoped for. She reported for the school newspaper, did well in her classes, and enjoyed the company of old friends.

"My pals Hazel, Annie, and I took turns [driving to school] with our horse and buggy," she recalls. "It was a wonderful term, and I had been assured by my teachers that with a little extra work I could make up the time lost in my second year and could graduate in 1912."

But it was not to be. Having no way to support herself, she was forced to live at home, where her stepmother became increasingly intolerable. She stuck it out, working on the family ranch through the summer, but finally in November of 1912 she called Earl Dodson, by now her fiancé, for help.

"I said, 'Well, let's get married. I cannot stand this any more,'" she recounts. The couple would try to support themselves by farming. Their son, Jack, was born in 1914, and three years later their daughter, Gene, followed.

Nellie Garner welcomed the news and replied with a breezy report on the modernization of Berry Camp, on September 2, 1917:

> We received your card, were glad to hear from you . . . The telephone sure is lots of company. Fine big bathroom hot and cold water all over and water piped into garden. Mr. Stade at the Central has a big, two-story building, some class. Miller House has a fine new building and Mr. Kelly on Miller Creek has a swell new house along with Pete Anderson's.

Nellie had apparently won a battle against sciatica rheumatism, but Ed developed serious eye problems that warranted medical help from outside the territory.

He has waited so long one eye certainly is awful, just as red as blood all the time and pains him so at night that he can hardly sleep.

Would love to see your new baby. Uncle Ed will likely get to see you all but I will not. I am going to stay in this winter and run the ranch. . . . It costs so much to go out and I just hate traveling anyway on the water . . .

This was the last letter Peggy saved from her adopted mother, and a bad omen, for the following year all three Garners—Nellie, Ed, and Alf—booked southern passage on the ill-fated *Princess Sophia* to visit family and purchase mining equipment.

The vessel was one of the newest of a proud fleet of the British Columbia Coast Steamship Service of the Canadian Pacific Railway Company—245 feet long, 44 feet wide with a gross tonnage of 2,320, built at a cost of about $250,000. In 1918 she was licensed to carry 250 passengers, but because it was close to freezeup with 600 to 700 people reported waiting to go south from Skagway, the *Princess Sophia* shipped on October 23 with about 350 passengers and a crew of 65.

At 2:00 a.m. the next day, for reasons never made clear, the ship, going eleven to twelve knots, hit Vanderbilt Reef in Lynn Canal off Juneau, lifting its bow out of the water, ripping a formidable hole in the bottom, and planting itself on solid rock.

Because of rough seas driven by a howling north wind, the captain decided it was unsafe to launch the lifeboats and refused to endanger rescuers. Instead, he and his passengers waited forty hours for calmer weather that never came.

Then, a few minutes before 4:50 p.m. on October 25, in blinding snow and pounding seas, the ship shifted 180 degrees and slid backwards off the reef. Rocks ripped gaping holes in her hull. The boilers exploded, killing many instantly. The rest died quickly, smothered in oil or stunned by near-freezing, dark waters.

The only survivor was an English setter that came ashore covered with oil at Tee Harbor, eight miles from the reef. When found two days later, the dog had struggled another four miles to Auke Bay.[54]

Nellie's body was shipped to the Rouches in California. "Only the sweet little face showed. Hands covered with gloves," Peggy remembers. "Alf's closed coffin arrived a day or so later with orders not to open." Ned's body was never found.

Another casualty, although not reported on the ship's manifest, may have been Rass Rassmussen, whom Peggy recalls died in a terrible shipwreck, "probably the *Sophia*."

Also aboard the *Sophia*, unbeknownst to Peggy, was the former "Miss Geer" with whom the Garner group had made their 1909 voyage north, who was traveling with her husband and uncle, a pioneer miner from the Fortymile named John Colver.

Peggy's mysterious, tight-lipped traveling companion, Olive Geer, daughter of a well-known Yukon riverboat captain, had married Albert D. Pinska, a native of St. Paul, Minnesota, who had gone to Dawson City in 1906 to manage a store owned by his brother, Martin.

The couple was widely known in Dawson and well liked. Olive was a member of the Women's Ambulance Corps and secretary of the Klondike Knitting Klub, which became a branch of the Red Cross during World War I. Her curling team had won a prize in Dawson for a patriotic bonspiel of 1917. Albert was an equally keen sportsman, a champion bowler and curler, as well as an expert knitter who helped his wife with her war effort, making socks for the troops.

The Pinskas had sold out in Dawson and were headed Outside with the patriotic hope that Albert might join the army. Chances were dim for him at age forty-five, but that failing, the couple hoped he would find work in a shipyard because the job market in Dawson was slipping.[55]

Also on the list of casualties were Pete Anderson, Peggy's would-be suitor who had become quite wealthy and apparently married happily. Usually the couple wintered in Fairbanks but in 1917, they elected to travel Outside, and Helen Callahan, who had worked for them the previous mining season, was devastated by news of their deaths.

She wrote in her diary, "Came to Fairbanks Oct 6 from Mastodon where I have been with Mr. and Mrs. Anderson since April 15. Last time I seen Mrs. Anderson Sept 20 little did I think I would never see her again when I left her. God bless them both, the best friends I ever had, both drowned on S.S. *Sophia* Oct 25, 1918. The three Garners from Eagle Cr. May God keep there [*sic*] souls."[56]

In the Far North, especially in sparsely populated Interior mining districts, it was the tragic end of an era. "Most of those who lost their lives on the *Princess Sophia* in Lynn Canal on that fatal morning of October 24 were the most prominent people of the Yukon Valley, both Americans and Canadians," the *Daily Alaska Dispatch* observed (October 26, 1918). With them went the dazzling future that had been the dream of early pioneers.

For Peggy, the loss capped a long nightmare. "My mother died when I was three. Then, later, my sister-in-law, pregnant at the time, fell off a ladder which caused the death of both she and her baby," she wrote. "My aunt, who had cared for me for several years, died of blood poisoning. My father died in an explosion."

But fortunately, Peggy now had a family of her own to invest in. Daughter Joyce, born in 1921, added to the Dodsons' happiness.

It wasn't all easy, of course. Earl Dodson was not cut out to be a farmer so Peggy took over, letting him focus on driving the tractor, welding, and inventing equipment. The family moved to southern California, back to Kingsburg where Earl ran a welding and machine shop, then to Santa Cruz and Campbell, finally to Carmichael. But at all these locations the Dodsons enjoyed their family life, and Peggy managed time for self education, garden and hiking clubs, Girl Scouts, writing classes, painting, and travel.

About the only thing Peggy Rouch Dodson didn't pursue was the keen marksmanship and love of hunting she inherited from her Uncle Alf. Early on, after she married, she and Earl faced the problem of dispatching a live turkey to cook for Thanksgiving dinner. Earl bet she couldn't shoot it in the head, and she dispatched it neatly, but it was the last time she ever shot.

Peggy and Earl enjoyed fifty-nine years of marriage before he died of heart failure in 1971. Son Jack, a building contractor in Kingsburg, California, had died two years earlier at age fifty-five. Joyce, a semiretired homemaker, and her husband, Bill, retired from the local power company, help take care of Peggy, who lives next door to them in Carmichael, California. Daughter Gene, a retired college teacher, and her husband, Pat, retired from the California Department of Agriculture, also live nearby.

Added to the clan are eight grandchildren, twenty-one great-grandchildren and four great-great-grandchildren, none of whom has ever been to Alaska. (Her daughter Joyce did visit.) Nor did Peggy ever return.

Celebrating her 103rd birthday in 1996, she still thinks fondly of the country, yet she has never regretted turning down the Alaskan marriage proposals her aunt found so intriguing. And time proved her judgment fortuitous in at least two out of three cases, for the luck of George Lorenz, who pursued her so eagerly, proved even worse than that of the ill-fated Pete Anderson.

About 1912, Lorenz followed Peggy to California in hopes, perhaps, of pressing suit one more time. Rass Rassmussen, headed Outside to visit his family in Minnesota, ran into George on the boat leaving Alaska. In casual conversation Rass mentioned he planned to visit Peggy at her family's California ranch.

"I live in Redding, and I'll come with you if you don't mind," Lorenz told him. "I'd like to see Peggy and the ranch, and soon."

The Rouch family made a big event of the visit, giving the men a complete tour of their 160-acre ranch, but Peggy was careful not to find herself alone with Lorenz, as in the past. She never heard from him again, but two or three years later was astonished to read in her local paper that he had committed suicide after a double murder. The victims were the stepdaughters of Lorenz's brother, Alfred. When the older, age seventeen, spurned his attentions, he shot her and her fifteen-year-old sister who tried to run for help.

"Do you wonder that I shuddered a bit when I read this in the Fresno paper?" Peggy wrote a friend. "I'd not only spent time alone with him, I'd gone hunting with him!"

Chris Harrington, the miner who had employed Peggy and her aunt before they moved to Eagle Creek and who had also proposed to Peggy during that period, apparently enjoyed better luck. While most of his neighbors (including the Garners) sold out to Clarence Berry because they didn't have the capital to launch full-scale mining ventures, Harrington continued to work as a full partner with Louis Hansen and on his own, establishing his many mining properties as lucrative producers. His sale of one-third interest in the operation to E. T. Barnette, well-connected founder of the booming city of Fairbanks in 1910, probably brought him good publicity, and he continued to mine the area until January of 1914 when he sold nineteen claims and fractions of claims to E. I. Jensen for an undisclosed amount. (Jensen then sold to the Berry company.)

At this point Harrington disappears from Circle Mining District records, but it should be noted that his last transaction was witnessed by Hortense Gardner and R. F. Lewis in San Francisco where, no doubt, he landed safely.

True to her vow to her friend Peggy, Helen Callahan never married, although she had many suitors (including a Canadian mountie) and led a rich, full life. The same year that Peggy left Eagle Creek, Helen traveled to San Francisco, living for a while with well-to-do friends of her family, but she was not happy there. After a brief stay at Circle, she teamed with her mother at Fairbanks on a very successful fur sewing business.

For a while she managed to keep in touch with Peggy, sending her a tiny pair of beautiful, beaded moose skin boots on the birth of her son. "They were colorful from foot to top," recalls Peggy, who recently gave the gift to the Central Museum. "Leather laces and white fur around the tops proved intriguing mysteries to tiny, exploring hands."

Helen loved children, eventually saved money to acquire some additional schooling, and for many years taught at the segregated Indian school at Fort Yukon. Then, when her grand-niece, Lee Burmaster, was orphaned at age four, Helen raised her with the help of Grandma Callahan.

Like her mother, Helen was thoroughly independent and progressive. She was probably the first Native woman in Interior Alaska to own her own car—a Willis Knight that she learned to drive after winning it in a raffle. And four decades later she was the first stockholder to sign up with the Doyon Native Corporation, a creation of the Alaska Native Claims Settlement Act of 1971.[57]

By 1916, there were more than seventy mines in the Eagle-Circle region, employing 265 men and producing more than $375,000 in gold.[58] Ten years earlier, geologists had predicted the region contained more than $200 million in gold.[59] At the time the Guggenheims were reported to be interested, but the big-time developers ultimately focused on less remote areas that produced more.

In 1922, residents of Circle Mining District, realizing they were being passed by, lobbied for improvements: "For the past twenty-eight years this region has been a continuous producer of gold, one of the largest producing camps in Alaska. Its transportation accommodations have been by river roads to Circle, on the Yukon River, some fifty miles from the mines," they noted in a petition to the Road Commission. "These mines, already located, will be steady producers for twenty-eight years more, under favorable conditions. But the completion of the railroad to Fairbanks and the extension of the White Pass Railway to Mayo silver district [in Yukon Territory] which has been announced, will eliminate the river traffic passing Circle. . . . These conditions, we believe, justify us in asking consideration in the matter of road construction, even taking precedent over other sections of the Interior of Alaska not adversely affected by the completion of the railroad."[60]

The railroad planned to the Mayo silver district never materialized, but the extension of the railroad to Fairbanks did stifle river commerce as the Circle miners had predicted. In 1927, the Territory of Alaska built a rudimentary summer road system, mainly to support mining interests that were engineering an enormous ditch in the area to bring water to Fairbanks. The Richardson Highway ran from Valdez at saltwater to Fairbanks, and the Steese Highway went on to Circle, but the Circle extension was never paved. Nor would the government build a spur road leading from it to Circle Hot Springs and its heavily mined Deadwood area. Frank Leach, owner of the Circle Hot Springs Lodge, finally built the spur himself, and it would be more than another six decades before winter maintenance was provided.

Today, ironically, the area is best known to the outside world not for gold production, but because the Yukon Quest International Sled Dog Race follows the Garners' old trail over Eagle Summit, which is usually the toughest stretch on the grueling marathon from Whitehorse to Fairbanks.

Early on, the Circle Mining District—so full of promise when the Garners and Berry moved in with their big mining operations—lost out to Fairbanks (area population is 82,428 today) as the industrial center of Interior Alaska.

Deadwood (originally known as "Hog'em" because original stakers filed too many claims under fictitious names) acquired a post office in 1906. Central, reported as a roadhouse on the trail to Circle City by the U.S. Geological Survey in 1898, attracted enough residents to take the post office from Deadwood in 1925, but its population has long fluctuated between 400 in the summer and 150 in the winter.

Circle City, "Paris of the North" and once the largest mining town on the Yukon, dropped from 144 residents in Peggy's day to a low of 50 in 1930 and has finally rebounded to just under 100. Circle Hot Springs, purchased from homesteader Cassius Monohan by Frank Leach in 1909, survived bankruptcy to become Circle Hot Springs Resort. In 1924, it boasted the first privately constructed airstrip in Alaska (now a 3,600-foot strip maintained by the state), and today its lodge with an Olympic-sized pool is a year-round tourist attraction.

By 1943, the U.S. Geological Survey estimated one million troy ounces of gold had been taken out of the Circle Mining District.[61] Diamonds, at least three of them, have since been discovered in the area, but certainly not enough to encourage that industry, and gold-mining remains the heart of the economy here after nearly a century.[62] Residents estimate that since the 1980s, the remote district has dumped more than $30 million annually into Fairbanks and the State of Alaska.[63]

Unlike most other mining areas in the state, changes in the Circle district have not been monumental. Pete Anderson's sole heir, Anders Johannsen of Padingtorp, Backabay, Sweden, sold Pete's claim to John August Anderson of Miller House in 1919 for an undisclosed sum. J. C. Garner, trustee for the estate of Alf Garner, sold Garner's mining interests to Gus Chisholm three years later for $2,000.

Garner's bad luck was apparently passed on to Chisholm, who got disoriented traveling his claims one winter in the mid-1920s, succumbed to hypothermia, and lost parts of his nose, ears, and fingers due to freezing. Still he stayed on, working the claims until his death sometime between 1950 and 1960.

Jay F. Kelly, to his astonishment, was erroneously reported lost on the *Princess Sophia*. He was in the district at the time and stayed there, eventually passing his mining interests on to Jay F. Kelly Jr., who died before his father. After his son's death, the claims reverted to Jay and from him went to Jay's daughter and son-in-law, then on to his grandson, Fred Wilkinson, who is still successfully mining the area.

Otto Bayless continued to mine in Circle until he got a job as foreman for the Alaska Road Commission in the 1930s, moving first to Livengood, then to Delta, and later to Fairbanks. However, his son, Howard, married Alice Robertson, and the couple mined on Chicken Creek where Alice, now a widow, is still in the business with their grandson.

Frank Warren, a grandnephew of Sam Warren who traveled with the Garner family in 1909, keeps that name alive in the Circle district, where he is well known for having discovered one of the region's first diamonds. He and his wife, Mary O'Leary Warren, granddaughter of Nels Rasmussen and Axenia Cherosky, ran a store and restaurant in Circle from 1956 to 1977, then

mined placer gold on Crooked Creek, before retiring to Fairbanks with a beautiful summer home in Central.

Nels Rasmussen died in 1921 as the delayed result of chest
injuries sustained while he was chopping wood, and his widow,
Axenia, helped support their large family by running the local
telephone company he had established just after Peggy left
the area.

William O'Leary, who came north in the Klondike rush from
a California dairy farm and married Mary Dalton, one of the
Rasmussens' daughters, stayed on in Circle to become a teamster like his father-in-law, and sons George and Ed O'Leary ably
carried on the family tradition. Eddie, who only recently retired
as a teamster, still drives occasionally and George, a trucker for
Sourdough Fuel, continues to work the same route over the
Steese Highway as his grandfather pioneered.[64]

Today the original Berry camp can still be seen from the
highway paralleling Eagle Creek, looking from a distance much
the same as when Peggy turned her back on it in the early
winter of 1910. Close up, though, it is derelict and probably
well beyond reclamation. Nellie and Ed's "new" cabin is still
standing, roof intact, but gone to collectors are the big range
and the zinc-covered table for bread-baking, along with the
phonograph Peggy helped carry over the pass, the little cuckoo
clock, fur robes, and fancy pillows. The storerooms remain
surprisingly orderly, but part of the kitchen floor has fallen into
the shallow storage cellar beneath it, and the rest will soon follow.

The claims bought by Berry on Mammoth, Mastodon, and
Eagle Creeks in 1906 are still in the possession of Berry Petroleum Company, now a multinational corporation but still owned
in part by the Berry family through Eagle Creek Mining and
Drilling. Mining continues on the property originally acquired

from the Garner family and on neighboring claims once owned by Chris Harrington and Pete Anderson.

Tundra berries are still good picking out at Mastodon. The Iceland poppies, fireweed, forget-me-nots, wild honeysuckle, penstemon, and Johnny-jump-ups that enchanted Peggy Rouch still tangle into beautiful natural gardens up on Eagle Crest, and delphinium bloom just outside Nellie Garner's kitchen door where she planted them more than eighty years ago.

The size of the area's caribou herds has dwindled, but a few animals are still out there, grazing on the hills. The ptarmigan are still good hunting. And down in the valleys, just as in Peggy's day, men are mining the creek beds, dreaming of better days ahead.

At this writing no one has yet discovered the main source of gold for the area—the hard rock mother lode from whence all the placer gold washed down. Many hope it's up there still: somewhere in Mastodon Dome backing the Garners' old site, the old-timers will tell you. And one day soon someone will find it.

—Lael Morgan
    Fairbanks, Alaska
    May 1996

APPENDIX B
NELL GARNER: THE WOMAN
WHO WAS BOUND FOR ALASKA

AMES A. MICHENER introduces his novel *Journey* with a photo
of Peggy Rouch Dodson's aunt, Mrs. Nellie Garner, taken
in Edmonton, Canada, in 1897. She is young and pretty,
but she looks deadly serious despite her jaunty "Buster Brown"
cap and her modish suit with its stylish leg-o-mutton sleeves,
peplumed jacket, and daringly short (eight inches short of ankle-
length) riding skirt.

Michener chose this photo, he tells us, because it was "so
evocative of the thousands of amateurs streaming north that
it registered profoundly, becoming for me the symbol of that
period." He had been unable to learn the name or place of
origin of the woman, and he wondered in his epilogue, "Reflec-
tions," if she might have starved to death on the bank of some
turbulent mountain stream she was powerless to ford. "On the
other hand, her portrait is that of a determined young woman,
a realist, and there is a chance she turned her back on the folly
and returned to Edmonton, from where she quickly departed
for her former home in Michigan or Ontario," he suggested.
"Or, being the resolute woman she seems, she could well have
gone down the Mackenzie, over the mountain divide, and on to
her destination."[65]

In his first version of *Journey* (which was originally planned
as part of his epic novel *Alaska*), Michener had no place for a
heroine. It was a man's tale, tied heavily to careful research.
But he writes that he could not get Nellie Garner's pensive photo

out of his mind. "She was my guide, my muse, my touchstone, and was so indelible that she kept fighting her way back onto my pages," he confessed.

Later he learned her name from the Provincial Archives of Alberta. A researcher there reported the photo had been taken in the studio of Ernest Brown in August of 1897; that its subject had come from Fresno, California, with a party of eighteen men; and that they had purchased eighty horses in Edmonton and headed out on the overland trail with a great determination to find the gold fields.

"That's all we know, but the phrases haunt me, for the questions are limitless," Michener concluded. "Was her husband, or brother, among the eighteen men? How did he allow her to go to Edmonton? And why in the world should she have gone there when Seattle was so much closer and was the start of a much simpler route? What happened to the horses? What happened to her?"[66]

Shortly after *Journey* was published in 1989, Peggy Dodson's editor, Pat Oakes, wrote Michener to let him know that Nellie Garner had been every bit as resolute as he had perceived her to be. That although her party had failed to get to the Klondike along the killing Edmonton Trail, she and her husband had persevered, finally striking it rich in Alaska.

"Incredible!" Michener replied. "I am gratified to learn that she turned out to be just as gallant and interesting as I had supposed, and I would be most grateful if you were to send me an advance copy of what you are publishing."[67]

Girl in the Gold Camp, however, is more about the equally resolute Peggy Rouch than her aunt, and we've left the account of Nellie Garner's early travels to another writer, Melanie J. Mayer, who detailed them splendidly in her classic, *Klondike Women: True Tales of the 1897–1898 Gold Rush.*[68] What follows is quoted from her book:

ON THE OVERLAND ROUTE

Nellie (Mrs. G. Ed) Garner of Fresno, California, was one of at least twenty-one women who were among the fifteen hundred stampeders on the various branches of the Edmonton trails.[69] The Garners left Edmonton August 24, 1897, with a group of twenty other stampeders from Fresno. They were, therefore, among the first to search for signs of the overland trail northward. An optimistic Nellie wrote to relatives back home about their warm reception in Edmonton.

> We left Edmonton at four o'clock this evening and traveled eight miles, to St. Albert. During all of the time it was raining very hard, and owing to the darkness and disagreeable weather we did not stop to camp, but went to the hotel.
>
> It seemed as though everyone in the town was at the hotel to welcome us, and before leaving Edmonton, by the way, a large crowd of well-wishers surrounded and gave us a sort of "Fourth of July reception." The ladies and gentlemen persisted in approaching and introducing themselves. They all wished us good luck and, of course, gave me plenty of advice as to what I must wear, how to wear it, etc.
>
> A couple of photographers took my pictures in different poses and attire, and a local author is going to write a book about our party. It will be illustrated.[70]

On their 120 pack animals the Fresno party carried two years' supply of provisions—a ton of goods per person. The Canadian government insisted on adequate

preparation by requiring each prospector to bring a
year's supplies into the territory. There would be no welfare
for ill-equipped gold seekers. Fortunately the Garners
had realized before setting off that their trek would
be considerably longer than the 700 miles their Fresno-
hired expedition leader had led them to believe. He, in
the meantime, skipped town with his "advance payments
of fees" as soon as they reached Edmonton.[71] According
to Nellie, their first few days on the trail were rather
festive.

> Tea parties were planned, and I received
> any number of invitations to attend them.
> All along the road and at stopping places
> people stare at our party, . . . and I often hear
> them say, "There goes the woman who is
> bound for Alaska." Perhaps I look somewhat
> odd in my attire as I sit astride my horse with
> spurs dangling from my shoes. We are travel-
> ing fifteen or sixteen miles each day, and if
> our present good health continues I think we
> shall reach our destination about the time
> we figured on.
>
> We had a guide with us. The kind-hearted
> people of Edmonton hired him to accompany
> us. The people of this part of the country
> make every inducement to those who wish
> to travel to Alaska by the overland route.
> They desire them to come this way.[72]

Buoyed by the holiday-like atmosphere that their
departure elicited, Nellie's only complaints in this early
letter were of frightful weather, of nearly losing one of
the horses in a river crossing, and of her annoyance with
cooking. According to the newspaper which published

portions of her letter, she alluded to her suffering and being nearly blinded by smoke.[73]

Three weeks later the Garners' party had progressed about one hundred miles, and they were struggling to get their horses through miles of fallen timber. A member of the party who turned back October 2 reported the following:

> We experienced the greatest difficulty in keeping our horses in condition. The feed is good and there is plenty of water, but the difficulties of the trail are death to horses. The trail is filled with spots called "muskeags" which are small marshes, covered for a few miles with moss. A horse, stepping on one of these, sinks to his body. It sometimes takes hours to get him out. Then again, the trail is blocked by fallen timber, thrown down by forest fires. It was necessary to jump the horses over this. Such work wore our horses out fast, and we were obliged to abandon many of them along the trail.
>
> We lost so many horses that it soon became evident that we could not all get through. I accordingly sold my remaining horses and outfit to T. J. Kelly, my partner. This will materially aid him in his journey to the diggings.[74]

Of course, such struggling by hundreds of impatient travelers also took its toll on the Canadian wilderness. Many stampeders on the overland trails seemed peculiarly unconcerned that they were, in fact, guests in someone else's land. They left smoldering campfires to burn trees and grasslands. They grazed pack animals in small meadows they found in the heavy forest, leaving little feed for wild animals or Native Americans' horses. They cut their way through forests and killed wildlife with thoughts only of reaching the Klondike. Some destroyed Indian traps and domestic animals as though they were entitled to eliminate anything that did not serve their purpose. It is not surprising that the stampede was not welcomed by many of the native populations of western Canada.[75]

When winter set in seventy-three days after they left Edmonton, the Garners were at Fort St. John on the Peace River, only 250 air miles from their starting place. By that time the Fresno party had added 94 of their 120 horses to the over 4,000 other animals that would eventually die on the Edmonton overland trails.[76] In the spring, eighteen of the original twenty-two stampeders set out again. They passed through Fort Grahame in mid-June, painstakingly cutting a pack trail through dense forest as they proceeded up the Fox River Valley. By mid-July of 1898 two members of the party were beginning to show signs of scurvy.

In those days it was not known generally that scurvy was caused by vitamin C deficiency, so few stampeders knew how to prevent it. Some theorized that it was caused by a poisoning, allied with ptomaine, from badly preserved fish and meat.[77] Proposed therapy included fresh fruits, vegetables, and meats, and some advocated exercise—something of which the stampeders had plenty. Marie Riedselle, a masseuse advertising in the June 28, 1898, *Klondike Nugget* even claimed, "Scurvy prevented and cured by new method. Lost vitality restored." Those who ate only the supplies they carried did not get vitamin C; as a result, many who were on the trails for long periods of time, as on the Edmonton routes, got scurvy. It was, in fact, the Edmonton trails' chief cause of death—claiming thirty-two of seventy who perished.[78] And scurvy is one of the slowest, most painful ways to die. First symptoms are innocent enough—aching muscles and bruised-looking skin. But then one notices that the flesh under the bruise is spongy rather than resilient. Gums become soft and bleed, teeth fall out, and eventually there is hemorrhaging from most mucous tissue. The victim gradually loses all energy, becoming unable to move, and finally welcomes the death that ends long months of suffering. If fresh food is eaten, however, recovery comes within a couple of days.

On July 24, 1898, then, Nellie Garner and members of her party recognized the seriousness of their companions' conditions. Though they were within a few miles of the Yukon River watershed, their progress was nevertheless too slow to continue safely. So Nellie and seven others in the party decided to turn back. She was very disappointed when interviewed by the editor of the Edmonton *Bulletin* on September 5, 1898. It had been over a year since she had set out for the Klondike. The editor wrote, "Mrs. Garner, though realizing that the trip was more arduous than she had ever expected, regrets the circumstances which compelled her husband's and her own return and was anxious to keep on and if necessary to go through to Dawson."[79]

Members of the Fresno party were not the only ones to be disappointed by the Edmonton trails. It was not uncommon to spend a year on the trail, and several parties took as long as two years, for those who survived. One account of this trail reports that "for every single man lost on the White and Chilkoot passes, hundreds perished on the Edmonton Trail."[80]

A more systematic study shows that the outcome was not so drastic. Of the approximately 1,500 people who set out from Edmonton, over 700 arrived in Dawson by 1899. Of the 775 who went overland, 160 reached Dawson and 35 are known to have died. Of the 785 who went by the water route, 565 got to Dawson and another 35 died along the way. The others either turned back before it was too late, or became settlers somewhere along the routes. However, this systematic study probably underestimates the number who died because it counts only confirmed deaths on the trail and does not include those who reached Dawson but died soon after from their efforts in the strenuous country.[81]

Michener was right in questioning what Nellie Garner was doing on the Edmonton route. The businessmen of that city who promoted it were criminally negligent, which is what Michener's novel *Journey* is all about. And the famous writer was also correct in guessing that his muse might be tough and determined enough to make it through to the gold fields, despite the perils of the Edmonton route.

Nellie Garner was an amazingly strong and courageous woman, and Peggy Rouch did well in choosing her as a role model and "mother."

—Lael Morgan

NOTES

1. Rasmus Rassmussen had family in Minnesota and does not seem to have been part of the California group with which the Garners usually traveled. His half-brother, Jens Peter Rasmussen, staked claims Nos. 2, 3, and 4 on Butte Creek, close to Eagle Creek, on January 17, 1898, and several other claims in the area about the same time, according to mining records. Peggy Dodson recalls Rasmus lived for some time with the Garners and that they all were extremely fond of him. In photos he appears to be Alf's age or slightly older.

    Mining records for 1909 show that Pete Anderson paid $4,199 to buy half-interest in two claims on Mastodon Creek from the Jens Rasmussen estate and that Nels Rasmussen was administrator of that estate, although we can find no signs that Nels was related to either Jens or Rasmus. (Note that Rass's last name was spelled "Rassmussen.")

    The last official mention we can find of Rass is on December 12, 1912, when, as "half brother and next of kin and sole heir of Jens Peter Rasmussen," he granted to Floyd T. Steele of Fairbanks the remainder of Jens's claims: Nos. 19 and 20, Mastodon, and claims Nos. 12, 13, and 15 on Miller Creek for $2,000. The transaction was made in Windsor, Ontario, Canada, and lists Rasmus as a resident of Walkerville, Essex, Ontario (Circle District Deed Book 2, 1900–1915: 410–411).

2. Nellie and Ned traveled the Edmonton Trail in 1897–1898 with a group known as the "Fresno Party," and M. Clark and Jim Woods may have been part of this group. J. M. Woods is listed as doing assessment work for Jay Kelly and his wife on Miller Creek in December of 1909, but beyond that, we can find no mention of either Jim or his nephew, Andy, in Circle Mining District records.

3.   Sam Warren appears to have been the only one of the Garner party who would eventually settle into the country for good. Although his name does not appear in later city directories or in miners' records for the next two decades, his descendants can still be found in Central.

4.   The *Cottage City*, which had been making the Seattle-to-Skagway run since the early days of the Klondike Rush, belonged to the Pacific Coast Steamship Company, which advertised both in the *Daily Alaska Dispatch* (Juneau) and the *Daily Star* (Whitehorse) in 1909. The steamship could make the round-trip run from Seattle to Skagway in nine or ten days.
      On January 27, 1911, the *Cottage City* ran into a rock near Cape Mudge, British Columbia, in a blinding snowstorm en route from Skagway. Passengers and crew were rescued, but the ship sank shortly after being abandoned.

5.   The girl was Olive Geer, the only daughter of Captain Joel P. Geer of the steamer *La France*, a pioneer Yukon River steamboat man whose brother, E. C. Geer, was one of Oregon's most noted governors. Another uncle on her mother's side was John Colver of Eugene, Oregon, a Klondike pioneer who was then mining on Chicken Creek in the Fortymile District of Alaska, which may be where Olive was headed when she left the Garners.
      Motherless from the time she was very young, Olive had traveled north with her father and taken a job with the North American Transportation and Trading Company (NAT&T), which had a branch at the settlement of Fortymile on the Canadian side of the border. During this period she was also traveling freely in Yukon Territory, staking mining claims, which was an unusual thing for a woman to do in that era. In October of 1909, the *Dawson Daily News* reported Miss O. K. Geer traveling with Miss R. Neilson on the stage from Dawson to Stewart Crossing, from whence Miss Geer would take a dog team for Barker Creek, south of Dawson in Yukon Territory.
      The following winter the Dawson paper reported "Olive Greer [*sic*] of Barker Creek passed through here on her way to Dawson. Miss Greer [*sic*] has proved herself quite a stampeder. She has staked in all the various stampedes that have taken place this winter" (February 28, 1910). In November of 1910, Olive's only brother, Earl,

was murdered during a native uprising on the island of Marandan in the Philippines, where he was running a plantation with his bride. Olive's father retired to Oregon shortly thereafter, but she stayed on in Yukon Territory.

6.   The narrow gauge White Pass & Yukon Railroad, connecting the town of Skagway, Alaska, to Whitehorse, Yukon Territory, Canada, was built between June 1, 1898, and October 1, 1900, at a cost of over $10 million. Backing for the venture came from the Close Brothers, a London banking firm, under the leadership of Michael J. "Big Mike" Henry, the most famous railroad man in the Far North.

7.   An extension of the White Pass & Yukon Railroad planned from Whitehorse to Dawson was never built. Instead, the company used sternwheelers to carry passengers and freight north, but many travelers like the Garners found it cheaper and/or quicker to provide their own transport from Whitehorse on the water route used by the first gold rush stampeders.

8.   "Klondike Kate" Rockwell was one of the most famous dance hall girls of the Dawson Gold Rush, not only because she was a good performer but also because of her knack for self-promotion. In the '30s, she sold her life story to a Hollywood moviemaker, and her exciting biography, *Klondike Kate: 1873–1957,* by Ellis Lucia, is still in print.

The magnate who threw her over was Alex Pantages, a bar waiter when she met him in Dawson, who built marvelous theaters all along the West Coast using Kate's earnings for his original stake. Whether or not he paid her back is a matter of debate. She died poor, and his success was marred by a fifty-year sentence in San Quentin for child molestation in 1929. He was freed after a second trial in 1931.

9.   Al may have been Albert "Mike" D. Pinska, who had come to Dawson from St. Paul, Minnesota, to manage a clothing store for his brother, Martin. It is not known when Olive Geer met Pinska, but the *Dawson Daily News* reported on June 9, 1909 (while she was traveling with the Garners), that he was playing baseball for a local team called the Pie Cards "picturesquely done up in blue effects, with a pair of mooseskin moccasins. . . ." Geer married him

sometime after 1912. Both Pinska and Geer were known as expert hunters and outdoor fans, which may be why Olive kept to herself with the ultra-cautious "sunbonnet" crowd.

It may seem strange that the Garner family did not learn more about the Geer girl, but it was (and still is) the unwritten etiquette of the Yukon not to ask questions if information was not volunteered.

10.   The name "Circle" was also a misnomer. Trader Leroy Napoleon "Jack" McQuesten, who located his trading post there in 1887, named it, thinking mistakenly that it lay on the Arctic Circle, when actually it is about fifty miles south.

11.   Frank Jewett was part-owner of Jewett and Dodson, a general merchandise store in Circle and an agent for North American Transportation and Trading Company (NAT&T), billed as "the pioneer merchants and carriers of Alaska," who controlled a healthy share of Yukon barge traffic in competition with the Northern Commercial Company (N. C.). Jewett also held many mining claims in the area. His wife was a nurse. In February of 1910 with the thermometer registering more than fifty below, F. J. Jewett and his wife made the 160-mile trip from Circle to Fairbanks by dog team so that Mrs. Jewett could have an emergency operation for appendicitis. The trip took them four days. Every jar of the sled brought wrenching pain, but Mrs. Jewett managed to get medical help and survive the operation.

12.   Even when Circle City's population stood at 1,000, there were only twenty white women recorded as residents in the entire Yukon Valley plus a few transient dance hall girls, "actresses," and prostitutes. By 1909, there was little incentive for transient women to visit, and wives made up the bulk of the white female population.

13.   Nels Rasmussen was apparently no relation of the Garners' family friend, Rass Rassmussen. The teamster emigrated from Copenhagen, Denmark, to Seattle, Washington, to work after hearing tales of jobs, gold, and excitement in Alaska. He was listed on gold-mining claims in the Rampart District as early as 1897, and in 1899 it is recorded that he sold an interest in the Palisades Coal Mine (115 miles downstream from Rampart).

In May of 1901, Rasmussen is listed in Rampart's newspaper, the *Alaska Forum,* as "guard at the bird cage [jail]." Also in that year he wed Axenia Cherosky, the daughter of Erinia Pavaloff and Cherosky Demoski (also known simply as "Cherosky"), one of the discoverers of Circle's first gold strike. The Rasmussens had eight children, and Nels built them a large, two-story house in Circle known to family and friends as "the Big House." (From funeral notes of Nels's daughter, Elsie K. O'Leary, taken June 14, 1994.)

In 1905–1906, Rasmussen, with several other owners on Deadwood Creek, deeded a gold claim to the Circle Alaska Mining Company. He made his living primarily as a teamster and was known locally as "the Mule King."

14.   During this era a close friendship between an Alaska Native and a white girl would have been frowned upon, but Helen Callahan was in a class by herself. Her Nulato-born parents were part Athabaskan, part Russian, a mix that became an elite class during the Russian occupation of Alaska. Helen's natural father, Cherosky Demoski, made the original gold discovery in that region on Birch Creek in 1891 with her uncle, Pitka Pavaloff. Then Helen's mother, Erinia Pavaloff, married Dan Callahan, who was at that time one of the wealthiest and most powerful men in Circle City and later in Fairbanks and would go on to serve in the territorial legislature. Nels Rasmussen's wife, Axenia, was Helen's sister.

15.   Called the "Paris of the North" in its heyday (1896–97), Circle City boasted a population of about 1,000 with 300 log cabins, several two-story buildings, twenty-eight saloons, a brewery, an "opera house," and a free circulating library. By the time Peggy arrived little more than a decade later, the population was officially recorded as 144, and the following January Al Garner told the *Fairbanks Daily Times* there were "only about twenty persons residing there."

16.   Gold was first discovered at Mastodon Creek on July 22, 1894 by John Gregor and Patrick Kinnely (also spelled "Kenneally" or "Kinnelly").

Chris Harrington's name does not appear on the mining records of this area until December of 1895, when he is listed as a witness to two sales by Frank Neumayer on Mastodon Creek to L. C. Brown and John Reese. The following year, A. Harrington sold claim No. 1 below to Charles Andrews. Another reference notes that Harrington was in the Birch Creek district in 1896 when mining was good. "Wages were $10 a day of 10 hours, and the operators were looking for men constantly. Gregor and Kenneally [Kinnely], Harrington and Herman . . . and scores of others made fortunes—and in many instances spent them," a writer for the *Fairbanks Daily Times* later recalled (August 29, 1906).

In July of 1897, Harrington, in partnership with George Herrman, bought out Andrews's interests for $2,500. (Herrman may have been G. W. Herrman, who is credited with the Poorman strike in the Ruby Mining District in 1912.)

Oddly, the next mention of Harrington comes from Dawson City, Yukon Territory, where, on June 14, 1898, A. Harrington bought claim No. 11 above, Eagle Creek, for $3,000 "out of mining proceeds." Since "Chris" Harrington filed that bill of sale for the claim with the Eagle Creek recorder on August 20 of that year, it is obvious Chris and A. Harrington were one and the same. It would seem that Harrington, like a large percentage of Circle miners, journeyed to Yukon Territory for the Dawson strike, but that he wasted no time in returning to Alaska, which was apparently a good decision.

When John Gregor, one of the original Mastodon discoverers, died in 1909, he left an estate valued at a quarter of a million dollars, and Mastodon continued to be a good producer. According to Donald Orth's *Dictionary of Alaska Place Names,* a post office operated there from 1902 to 1906, when the rush apparently began to subside.

At this point, Harrington sold two claims on Eagle Creek and turned his attention to assessment work on an "old channel" bench claim at the junction of Mammoth and Mastodon with Louis C. Hansen as his partner.

On July 21, 1909, the *Fairbanks Times* noted "Herrington & Hanson [*sic*] have a hydraulic plant in operation on Mastodon Creek and a large crew of men at work. This concern owns about a mile of ground and expects to take out a large amount of money." On December 31, the paper reported Harrington and Hansen getting lumber to build a 4,000-foot flume to get high water to their bench "which will require over ten years to work out." One year later, Harrington parleyed that publicity into the "sale" of one-third interest in seven of his Mastodon Creek claims to E. T. Barnette, the founder of the mining town of Fairbanks. The price recorded was one dollar, but Barnette was incredibly well-off and well-connected at that time, and we can only imagine what he offered to tempt Harrington to sell.

According to the *Fairbanks Daily Times* for May 4, 1910, Harrington was well known in Fairbanks:

"Loaded down with 1,000 pounds [it does not say pounds of what] of Mammoth creek above Miller House on the Circle Trail, together with three dozen wild geese bagged in the same section, Chris Herrington [*sic*] has just arrived in the city from Mastodon Creek with the result that many of his friends are today tasting the fresh fruits of Nature's larder.

"Dan Callahan [then a Fairbanks city councilman and well-heeled, fast-living property owner] carried a broad smile yesterday, for he announced that those geese certainly looked good in the oven."

17.   Nellie had minor surgery and hadn't been feeling too well.

18.   Henry "Old Man" Stade (pronounced "stead"), cook at the Jump Off and Central, was most remembered for twirling his beard with a fork and then using the same fork for cooking. Old-timers also recall he was careless about letting his cat get in the food, but he seemed to do very well in business. Stade probably came into the area with the first wave of prospectors, for he served as recorder for the first claims on Miller Creek on May 25, 1895.

Early the next year, Stade was deserted by his mail-order bride, who moved twenty-two miles north of their roadhouse at Jump Off to Circle, where she opened a laundry. Stade's reaction is not recorded, but Mrs. Stade was murdered, apparently by Frank White, a stationary engineer from Dawson.

White had been a frequent caller on Mrs. Stade, as had another resident of that camp. "It is believed that White killed the woman because she favored the suit of the other man rather than his own," the *Fairbanks Daily Times* reported on February 26, 1910.

The *Dawson Daily News* reported, "White armed himself with a 30-30, and followed Mrs. Stead to the Marshall's home where he found her alone. He fired three shots into her body, killing her instantly, and then he shot his own fool head off. When [Marshall] Irons reached home, he found his residence full of dead people."

Mrs. Stade, whose first name was never given, was taking care of a grandchild at the time of her death. Her age was given as "about fifty" and that of her would-be suitor as thirty-five, which would lead one to believe that female companionship was indeed hard to come by.

Henry Stade apparently did not remarry but went on to prosper. Quite along in years, he eventually sold the Central Roadhouse to Riley Ericksen and later died in a Masonic Home in Zenith, Washington, according to the recollections of Mary Bayless.

19. Jump Off was a tiny settlement with a lumber mill north of Central and twenty-two miles south of Circle City, where Nels Rasmussen once pastured his horses and ran a roadhouse. It got its name because it was the change-over point off Birch Creek, an area of considerable mining activity, where supply boats could dock at high water. The U.S. Geological Survey (USGS) reported a roadhouse still there at the junction of Jump Off Creek and Crooked Creek in 1915.

20. Twelve Mile House, located on Birch Creek, twelve miles southwest of Circle, was the site of a mining camp established in 1896. The roadhouse was apparently established about 1903.

The name "Central House" was reported in 1896 by the USGS as a roadhouse on the trail to Circle. Bill and Molly Bayless owned it in the early 1900s. Stade bought half-interest in it from Gus Ranson for $2,750 in July of 1912. The Baylesses probably owned the other half but records are missing.

Old-timers recall William "Bill" Bayless sitting at the Central Roadhouse telling tall tales and then saying to his wife, "Ain't that so, Molly?" She always replied "I don't remember," because she did not want to agree or disagree with him.

21.   Charles "Chas" Lamb originally went to Fortymile with Clarence Berry and made a big strike in Dawson about the same time Berry did. Unlike Berry, Lamb had gone to Klondike without his wife and, according to family legend, he returned to stack a large pile of gold on the table in front of her as a surprise.

Peggy recalls that Lamb and his wife were in partnership with the Berrys when she arrived. According to the *Fairbanks Times,* July 21, 1909, "Charles Lamb has just completed a large two-story residence which will compare favorably with the best houses in this city, and quite a town has grown up about the old roadhouse, in consequence of the new lease on life given the old gold producer."

Peggy's photo collection includes several pictures of the Garners, Lambs, and Mildred Kelly on the porch of this new house, which later came to be known as the Berry House.

22.   The family made a classic photo of this event, carefully preserved in this book and, at well over 100 years of age, Peggy still recalls the brand name of the horn: "Morning Glory Bell." The phonograph that they purchased was a "modern" one that used flat records instead of the round wax cylinders that first came on the market.

23.   Although the windswept area in which they mined and built was virtually treeless, there was a fine stand of timber in a sheltered area at Mastodon Fork, a short distance away.

24.   Butte Creek was about five miles southwest of the Berry camp on Eagle Creek. Under the law of that time, miners were required to do at least $100 worth of assessment work annually to hold a claim.

25.   Because the Berry claim was not being worked by a large number of hands, was farther off the beaten path than Harrington's, and attracted far fewer guests, Nellie may have felt more secure in letting Peggy off on her own.

26. Nellie and Ed Garner had "camped" most of their married lives. This would have been their first real home in Alaska.

27. The newspaper of January 11, 1910, lists a Captain Bowman from Birch Creek, and mining records show him to be N. A. Bowman who in 1910 sold a one-eighth interest share in Corinne, Butte, Nevada, and Victorine associations on Frying Pan Creek, a tributary of Birch. The next year he and A. E. Murphy offered C. J. Stewart one-half interest in the Eagle Association, Big Four Association, and Afterthought Association (on Eagle Creek) for $20,000. The last mention of him is in 1921, when he deeded interests in seven sizable mining ventures on Eagle, Birch, Gold Dust, and Butte Creeks to H. A. Weir of Fairbanks.

28. Mrs. W. K. Dodson, the Circle City postmistress, was no relation to Earl Dodson, the man Peggy later married. She may have been the mother of three Dodson men, believed to be brothers, who came to the area from Dawson in the late 1890s. A note on one photo taken in 1908–1909 refers to Mrs. W. K. as the senior Mrs. Dodson.

John R. Dodson was a partner in the firm of Jewett & Dodson in Circle and also served as mining recorder there. An early Dawson paper reported that a man by that same name got "one of the good claims on Bonanza Creek."

J. W. Dodson (who may have been known as "Windy Jim" in Dawson) located Claim No. 1 and Discovery Claim on Pitka's Bar, June 19, 1900, which is where Pitka and Cherosky first struck gold before the turn of the century. One clipping notes J. W. Dodson went Outside to see family in Oregon in 1909. An old-timer writing to Pat Oakes recalls J. W. was a freighter and a mail carrier.

R. M. Dodson (probably Robert) is listed in *Polk's Directory* for 1909–1910 as postmaster, U.S. commissioner, and general merchandiser at Circle. He is also listed as recorder on a Deadwood transaction on January 11, 1911. One of Pat Oakes's old-timers wrote that R. M. left Alaska about 1910 to work in Washington and Oregon and eventually worked for Pendleton Mills. An unattributed note in his Central Museum file says the family was at Circle in the 1890s through 1910 or later, then in southwest Washington state.

29. The *Fairbanks Daily News* reported on December 31, 1909, that J. P. (John Peter) Anderson was one of twenty or thirty miners adding to their pile of pay dirt at Mastodon that winter. The writer also noted Nels Rasmussen was delivering 150 cords of wood to Anderson's mining property because the miner had ambitious plans for the summer ahead. On January 11, 1910, Anderson is listed as being from Miller House. On January 5, 1911, it was reported that Anderson, an individual miner on Mastodon, was shipping in a mining plant. And, according to the *Dawson Daily News* (September 7, 1911), Anderson finally struck pay dirt.

30. The event actually made social news in Fairbanks. According to an article in the *Fairbanks Daily Times,* January 11, 1910:

> At Eagle Creek Mrs. J. E. Garner, assisted by her niece, Miss Bertha Rousch [*sic*] and Miss Ellen [*sic*] Callahan of Fairbanks, had lavishly prepared for a Christmas entertainment and all the guests united in declaring it an immense success; everything from decorations to food and fun having been carefully planned and carried out.

> Mr. Nels Rasmussen, who was the popular conductor of the ladies, stated that never had a larger party of ladies crossed the Eagle summit and, as would be expected, the summit lived up to its reputation in making the trip both coming and going as disagreeable as could be, without being dangerous on account of the wind . . .

Peggy recalls they entertained forty people during that holiday, somehow squeezing them all in for a sit-down dinner at two long, narrow tables with a Christmas tree between them, with everyone dressed to the hilt.

31. Mrs. C. F. (Elizabeth) Griffith owned Miller Roadhouse at that time. Charles "Cap" Griffith is shown at Miller House in a Garner family photo with Frank Miller, and C. F. (Charles Fremont) Griffith is listed as doing assessment work on Loper Creek, a tributary of Preacher Creek in the Circle District, in 1909.

Although Peggy did not mention it in her account of traveling from Harrington's to the Garners' spread at Eagle Creek, she had to pass Miller House, which was on the main trail between Central and the Garners'. Originally built as Mammoth House by Fritz Miller and Casper Ellinger about 1896, it was taken over by Jay Kelly, who found it empty and decided it had been deserted, about 1902, according to Miller family recollections. Miller and Ellinger eventually returned to challenge Kelly in miners' court. The decision was that Kelly could have the property if he paid the original builders $1,000.

Land records show Griffith purchased the property from Charles McDonald of Valdez for $100 in 1909 and sold it to Jay Kelly for $3,000 in 1912. Another bill of sale shows Kelly purchased Ingwold Anderson's interest in Miller House for $5,000 in March of 1918.

The *Fairbanks Times* notes on July 21, 1909, that "quite a town has grown up about the old roadhouse, in consequence of the new lease of life given to the gold producer":

> Many of the old timers have turned their attention to quartz and are scattered through the hills to the east of the old diggings in search of ledges, where many promising outcroppings have been discovered.

> On the Harrison Creek side [about ten miles south of Miller House] are between thirty and forty miners and the outlook for this section is very encouraging, the ground being shallow and easy to work.

The next winter the *Fairbanks News* (November 5, 1909), reported Sidney Drake was opposed in renewal of his liquor license at Miller House on the grounds that it was unlawful to conduct a bar in an unpoliced community having a population of fifty or more persons within a radius of two miles. The bar stayed open, so apparently the community got a policeman.

32. Northern Commercial Company, a department store and heavy equipment dealer represented throughout early Alaska, was generally referred to as "N. C."

33. It was long the tradition in Alaska to leave doors open with food and fuel handy for those who passed by in need. Only in recent years with the invasion of marauding snowmachiners, four-wheeler

drivers, and other outsiders who steal, trash, and loot have locks appeared on the doors in bush outposts.

34. The Garners must have enjoyed the trip because in the winter of 1912 they were managing Circle Hot Springs, according to an account by Gertrude Bly, who was connected with neighboring Miller House. Later photos show Nellie happily gardening there, probably the following summer. Ed also continued at Eagle Creek for Berry.

35. Jay Franklin Kelly was born in Ohio in 1860 and apparently came into the country early with his wife, Mildred. They located and filed on claims Nos. 7, 6, 5, and 4 below Discovery on Miller Creek in 1903, and shortly thereafter Jay purchased No. 1 above Discovery. Sometime during this period, Kelly found Miller House to be deserted and, thinking it had been abandoned, established the roadhouse. (See note 31.)

36. Harry H. Mortensen first shows up in the Circle mining records in September of 1909 as locator of claim No. 6 below Independence Creek. In June of 1910 he optioned several claims in that area to Chris Harrington, finally selling to him in 1912. Deadwood was the heavily mined area between Central and Circle Hot Springs around the turn of the century. It may have gotten its name because permafrost badly stunts trees there.

37. Will and George Lorenz went to work for Charles Lamb in the spring of 1909 according to the *Dawson Daily News,* May 22, 1909. The paper reported the men were hydraulic experts from California and had departed that morning with four horses and double enders for "Birch Creek country where the party will start extensive hydraulic operations on Mastodon and Eagle Creeks . . .

"Lamb and Berry have twelve miles of hydraulic ground on Mastodon creek and the preliminary work carried on there last year has proved beyond doubt that they have a rich proposition. C. J. Berry has about four miles of the same character of ground on Eagle and work will be done at both places." The Lorenz brothers were to take charge of the work being done, according to the *Daily News.*

38. Anderson was determined to marry Peggy. He proposed to her repeatedly that year. The answer was always "No!"

39.   The Garners must have seen Pete Anderson as a man whose star was about to rise. "Pete Anderson, who went to Circle on a shoe-string after leaving Dawson, is the greatest miner of the bunch. He swims in gold," the *Fairbanks Daily News* would later report. "He did not get it by luck, but by good judgment and management" (September 7, 1911).

40.   Earl Dodson, the boy from "back home," whom Peggy fancied.

41.   Earl's uncle, Luther M. Dodson, ran a candy store in Fairbanks. Peggy met him later in Selma, California, but had no contact with him while in Alaska.

42.   According to her private correspondence, Peggy entertained three proposals of marriage while in Alaska. One was from mine owner Chris Harrington, for whom she and her aunt had worked out at Mastodon Creek, who was even more wealthy than Pete Anderson. But even with Earl, whom she loved, Peggy was reluctant to give up her independence, which women usually had to sacrifice at the altar during that era.

During this period, Alaska women had more freedom than most. In 1900, the women of Nome, Alaska, became the first in the territory to whom voting rights were extended (twenty years before passage of the Nineteenth Amendment), and voting rights were extended to them throughout the territory in 1913. Still, marriage certainly limited a woman's options.

Peggy's friend Helen Callahan also showed keen awareness of this in her private diary. Noting a friend's husband had gone on a "toot," she wrote, "lordy me ain't I glad I am not married to have to put up with anything like that . . . believe me I'll stay clear of that matrimony business."

43.   Pete Anderson's bad luck was to continue. That spring, he was out trying to open up an "aggravating piece of ground" when a tenacious fire broke out in his cabin, according to an account in the *Fairbanks Daily Times,* March 23, 1910:

> The roof eventually ignited from the stovepipe about the encircling timbers and burned without opposition until it had destroyed the cabin and mess house attached. The cache

contained about $1,200 worth of supplies and the loss [of these] taken with all the prospector's bedding, household paraphernalia and personal efforts, is a heavy blow.

Mr. Anderson knew nothing of his loss until he returned home after his day's labors and found his house and substance a mass of blackened ruins.

44. Jimmy McCarthy had entered into a "grubstake agreement" in 1907 to prospect on Birch Creek for E. M. Carr, Harold Preston, B. T. Carr, M. A. Gottstein, A. R. Heilig, L. W. Heilig, and C. C. Heid. E. M. Carr, a Seattle lawyer and partner with former Washington governor John McGraw, owned one of the richest and longest producing gold claims in Rampart and was, at one time, the U.S. commissioner in Fairbanks. McCarthy was one of Carr's partners in the Nevada Association, a 160-acre venture on Birch Creek, at the time of his death. Carr went on to become counsel for the Great Northern Railroad.

45. Peggy may have gotten the impression that Helen's adopted father was dead, but Helen's mother had simply divorced him, successfully claiming most of his property in a settlement that astonished the teamster. She was probably one of the first Native women in Alaska to officially dump a white spouse and most certainly the first to walk off with a major property settlement.

46. "Hooch" Albert was Albert Fortier, well known in Circle for making bootleg whiskey, mostly from dried fruit and some local berries. His brew sold for an unusually high price of seventy-five dollars a gallon, and according to legend, the stuff was "so hefty that after a few drinks one could easily sit on top of a glacier all day." He was also known for his ice cream, which may have explained his friendship with the Garners.

Fortier came to Alaska in 1884 and settled in Juneau. Four years later, traveling with saloon-keeper Bill McPhee, he located in Fortymile. Later he spent time in Circle, then traveled to Dawson during the stampede. Fortier settled in Fairbanks shortly after the town was founded in 1902, but in later years spent the bulk of his time in the Circle area (*Dawson Daily News,* July 1, 1911).

Hooch was certainly a friend of the Garners. There are several photos of him in their collection, including one of him playing the banjo in their living room with "Mr. Green" on the trombone.

47. Organized labor was moving into Fairbanks during this period, and there was occasional violence. Peggy recalls that the furniture was damaged there, before being sent on to Circle.

48. A "cleanup" happens when a miner cleans out the gold trapped in the bottom of his or her sluice box.

49. There were no women buried in the old cemetery at Central and only three at Circle. Old-timers will tell you that is not because women in that area enjoyed better health but because very few ever lived there. (See note 12.)

50. On July 6, 1911, the *Dawson Daily News* reported that "Hooch" Albert Fortier had recently made a great cross-country trip from Dawson, through Fortymile, Circle, and other camps to Fairbanks. According to the report, Fortier came from Birch Creek country, where he had been representing claims and prospecting during the winter.

   On October 6 of that year, the *Seattle Times* reported he was enjoying that city after twenty-seven years of life within the Arctic Circle. The reporter also noted Fortier had rheumatism and would be taking treatment there.

51. *Fairbanks Daily Times,* March 14, 1911.

52. The book is *Tundra: Romance and Adventure on Alaska Trails,* 1930. See pages 149–151, 162–163, 196–200, 234–243, 332–333.

53. Kelly met Edith Arlberg on a trip over the Valdez-Fairbanks trail, where she was cooking in a roadhouse. Before his first wife died, Edith cooked for the couple at Miller House. After her marriage to Kelly, Edith bore him two children, Madoline and Jay Franklin Kelly Jr.

54. A great source on this disaster is *The Sinking of the Princess Sophia: Taking the North Down With Her* by Ken Coates and Bill Morrison (Fairbanks: University of Alaska Press, 1991).

55. *Dawson Daily News,* November 7, 1918.

56. From a copy of Helen Callahan's diary at the Central Museum.

57. Interview with Lee Burmaster Alder, Fairbanks, Alaska, August 3, 1995.

58. Melody Webb, *The Last Frontier: A History of the Yukon Basin of Canada and Alaska* (Albuquerque: The University of New Mexico Press, 1985), page 283.

59. "Guggenheims Are Headed This Way," *Fairbanks Daily Times,* August 29, 1906.

60. Claus Naske, *Paving Alaska's Trails: The Work of the Alaska Road Commission* (University Press of America, 1986) page 92.

61. *Gold Placers of the Circle District, Alaska—Past, Present, and Future,* U.S. Geological Survey Bulletin, 1943, page 2.

62. George O'Leary and Earl Beistline, interviews in Fairbanks, October 1995.

63. Taken from a 1986 report produced by Pat Oakes, pleading for year-round maintenance of the road from the Circle Mining District to Fairbanks.

64. Interview with George O'Leary, Fairbanks, October 1995.

65. James A. Michener, *Journey: A Novel* (New York: Random House, 1989), page 224. Originally published in Canada in somewhat different form by McClelland and Steward in 1988.

66. *Journey,* pages 243–244.

67. Letter from James A. Michener to Patricia Oakes, October 20, 1989.

68. Melanie J. Mayer, *Klondike Women: True Tales of the 1897–1898 Gold Rush* (Swallow Press/Ohio University Press, 1989), pages 29–33.

69. J. G. MacGregor, *The Klondike Rush Through Edmonton, 1897–1898* (Toronto: McClelland and Steward, 1970), pages 245, 263. One other woman, Isadore Fix, might be added to MacGregor's tally. She is mentioned in the text (page 166) but is omitted from the list on page 263. Her marital status is not given. It can be assumed that Mrs. Sam Brown listed by MacGregor is the same as

Mrs. Braund whom Emily Craig Romig reports meeting in *A Pioneer Woman in Alaska.* Although some details about them vary, their stories are very similar. Mrs. Braund was traveling with her husband, and according to E. C. Romig, bore a baby at Fort McPherson on January 6, 1899. They got as far as Fort Yukon, then went to St. Michaels instead of Dawson. (Mayer's note 3, Chapter 2.)

70.   Fresno *Daily Evening Expositor,* September 23, 1897, page 1. (Mayer's note 4.)

71.   Fresno *Daily Evening Expositor,* August 4, 1897, page 1; September 4, 1897, page 8. (Mayer's note 5.)

72.   Fresno *Daily Evening Expositor,* September 23, 1897, page 1. (Mayer's note 6.)

73.   Ibid. (Mayer's note 7.)

74.   J. Wilbur Cate, in Fresno *Daily Evening Expositor,* October 28, 1897, page 1. (Mayer's note 8.)

75.   MacGregor, pages 201ff. (Mayer's note 9.)

76.   MacGregor, page 5. (Mayer's note 10.)

77.   Juneau *Alaska Searchlight,* March 27, 1897, page 3. (Mayer's note 11.)

78.   MacGregor, page 236. (Mayer's note 12.)

79.   Edmonton *Bulletin,* September 5, 1898. (Mayer's note 13.)

80.   Elizabeth Page, *Wild Horses and Gold* (New York: Farrar and Rinehart, 1932), page xi. This is an excellent, novelized account of one party's struggles to reach the Klondike by the Edmonton overland trail. (Mayer's note 14.)

81.   MacGregor, pages 233–236. For an account of one who died after arriving in Dawson, see W. Galpin, "Who Is to Blame?" in A. R. Crane, *Smiles and Tears from the Klondyke* (New York: Doxey's, 1901), pages 119ff. (Mayer's note 15.)